Hope Triumphs over Chaos

The La Plata Tornado of April 28, 2002

Anthony G. Puzzilla

Printed in the United States of America
ISBN: 978-1-7345504-4-3 (paperback)
ISBN: 978-1-7345504-5-0 (ebook)

Canoe Tree
Press

4697 Main Street
Manchester Center, VT 05255
Canoe Tree Press is a division of DartFrog Books

Front Cover Photograph: Aerial view of the horrific damage in the downtown business and residential area of La Plata looking northwest on April 29, 2002. This region was alternately battered with F3 and F4 force winds. The photograph was taken by James M. Thresher for *The Washington Post*.

Contents

Dedication

This book is dedicated to Mr. William F. Eckman, the former Mayor of the Town of La Plata, Maryland, the people of my beloved Town, and the multitude of volunteers who turned chaos into hope, and hope into another Triumph of the Human Spirit.

CHAPTER 1

The Town of La Plata

The Years, 1927-2002

The years following the deadly F4 La Plata tornado on November 9, 1926 brought rapid growth and prosperity to the town. In 1940, the completion of the Harry W. Nice Memorial Bridge heralded the entry of US 301 into southern Maryland. This major transportation development heralded the influx of businesses, commerce and people into the area. Extended from La Plata, US 301 heads south across the Potomac River into Virginia, eventually reaching Richmond.

To the north, US 301 passed through Waldorf before intersecting US Route 50 near Bowie. At that location, one can take US 50 east past Annapolis and cross the Chesapeake Bay Bridge to the Eastern Shore of Maryland. Maryland Route 6 is the main east-west highway serving La Plata, following Port Tobacco Road and Charles Street through town. From La Plata, MD 6 heads west to Port Tobacco and continues east to Charlotte Hall.

The destruction of La Plata's only elementary school in 1926 resulted in the establishment of two new Catholic schools, Sacred Heart and the Archbishop Neale School, which would have its own tragic encounter with the next F4 tornado to hit La Plata in 2002. Public schools in La Plata included La Plata High School, Milton Somers Middle School, Walter Mitchell Elementary, and Mary Matula Elementary. The portion of town west of Route 301was zoned for the James Craik and Maurice J. McDonough schools.

The La Plata downtown business area was developed in order to meet the needs of the growing population which would reach six-thousand, five-hundred forty-two people by the year 2000. Many small family businesses developed over the years, as well as a number of shopping centers including a major one located at the intersection of Routes 301 and 6, which included a large Safeway and CVS Pharmacy.

In 1926, the aforementioned F4 tornado cut through Charles County leaving many dead and injured. At the time, there was no medical facility in the vicinity. This event motivated the county leadership to establish the Civista Medical Center in order to serve the health needs of the county residents. In 1939, four-hundred eight patients were served at the hospital.

In 1970, the defunct Baltimore and Potomac Railroad to Pope's Creek was taken over by CSX Transportation, which began running a coal train to the Morgantown Generating Plant, using the Pope's Creek Subdivision rail line track. The facility consists of two base-loaded 624 MW coal-fired steam generating units, four 65 MW oil-fired peaking combustion units, and two 18 MW black start peaking turbines. The two coal-fired units are base-loaded supercritical steam units which became operational in the years 1970-1971.

A number of churches came into existence beginning in 1927, and two of them were directly impacted by the passage of the 2002 tornado. A number of volunteers affiliated with these churches in other Maryland counties and states, came to assist the people of La Plata by clearing debris from their homes. The St. Ignatius and United Methodist Churches had already provided their cemeteries as the final resting place for six of the young children killed in the 1926 tornado.

Baptist
First Baptist Church
9070 Hawthorne Rd, La Plata, MD 20646

Catholic
Sacred Heart Roman Catholic Church
201 St. Mary's Ave., La Plata, MD 20646

St. Ignatius Catholic Church
8855 Chapel Point Road
Port Tobacco, MD 20677

Church of the Nazarene
New Life Wesleyan Church
9690 Shepherds Creek Pl, La Plata, MD 20646

Episcopal
Christ Church (Port Tobacco Parish)
110 E Charles St, La Plata, MD 20646

United Methodist
La Plata United Methodist Church
3 Port Tobacco Road, La Plata, MD 20646

In other to ascertain the actual preparedness of Charles County, on April 28, 2002, I examined the in-depth and authoritative article, *An examination of preparedness, response, and recovery for the La Plata, Maryland tornado*, written by Robert M. Schwartz, PhD. The article appeared in the *Journal of Emergency Management*, Volume 1, Number 3, Fall 2003. "The Sheriff's Office has a manual that sets forth the rules, policies, and procedures for EM personnel. The manual is to be used in coordination with and subordinate to the Charles County Emergency Operations Plan (EOP). The manual details county, agency, and Sheriff's Office responsibilities, alerts and warnings, search and rescue, and evacuations related to disasters stemming from natural or anthropogenic causes. According to the manual, Charles County is vulnerable to meteorological events such as hurricanes, blizzards, ice storms, flooding, dam failures, tornadoes, wind storms, and drought. The manual calls for planning to mitigate the effects of these hazards, as well as duties related to these types of incidents for law enforcement: traffic control, security at designated facilities, evacuations, and search and rescue. The Local Emergency Planning Committee (LEPC) for Charles County is involved in the preparation and response of the EOP. This plan meets state and federal guidelines and is coordinated with the appropriate agencies. One LEPC document, the *Citizen's guide to emergency preparedness: Preparing a plan for emergency events*, contains a section on tornadoes. Furthermore, Dr. Schwartz observed, "The sirens in Charles County date back to the Cold War era of the 1960s and were used primarily for fires. They did not function for severe weather."

The Emergency Activation System (EAS) is used by television and radio stations to broadcast emergency alerts to the public. The National Weather Service (NWS) activates the EAS for the media with text or audio messages sent through NOAA Weather Radio (NWR). Many radio stations in Charles County are run remotely on weekends. If the Emergency Activation System (EAS) has a problem, there is no human being to correct the situation. Communication with the NWS is by hardline telephone with no backup system. **(In fact, the EAS failed during the tornado as no watches or warnings were ever transmitted to many radio stations in Charles County during the entire evening passage of the tornado).**

The spotting network for identifying and tracking tornadoes is limited in Charles County and is especially lacking in the western side of the county. Charles County, along with Prince George's and St. Mary's Counties, rely on volunteers for this service. Since storms move west to east, this is where the majority of the storms enter the county.

CHAPTER 2
The Tornado's Development and Approach

The September 2002 National Weather Services (NWS)' *Service Assessment* entitled **La Plata, Maryland Tornado Outbreak, April 28, 2002,** was used as the authoritative source of meteorological information used in this book. This report was prepared under the auspices of the Department of Commerce (DOC) and the National Oceanic and Atmospheric Administration (NOAA).

Tornadoes along the Atlantic coast are not common, and tornadoes of this severity (F4) are extremely rare. Only six F4 tornadoes have occurred farther north and east of the La Plata storm: Worchester, Massachusetts – 1953; New York/Massachusetts – 1973; Windsor Locks, Connecticut – 1979; five counties in New York – 1989; New Haven, Connecticut – 1989; North Egremont, Massachusetts – 1995. However, none of these tornadoes were as close to the coast as the 2002 La Plata storm. The tornado traveled across the Chesapeake Bay reaching almost to the Atlantic Ocean, a distance of a mere 30 miles. As far as severity and sheer destruction, only the June 9, 1953 Worchester tornado was more intense.

The weather system spawning the La Plata tornado of April 28, 2002, began developing in the Midwest a day earlier. The DOC/NOAA/NWS **Weather Forecast for Saturday, April 27, 2002** forecasted severe thunderstorms possible for the entire area.

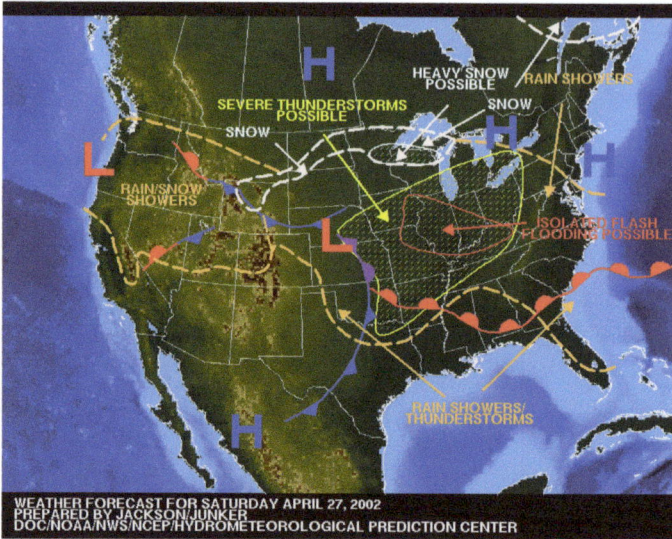

2-1: *The weather forecast for April 27, 2002.*

This system would continue to move eastward into the Ohio Valley and along the Mid-Atlantic States. The DOC/NOAA/NWS **Weather Forecast for Sunday, April 28, 2002** forecasted severe thunderstorms possible for the entire region.

2-2: *The weather forecast for April 28, 2002.*

A composite NOAA graphic from 7 a.m. EDT on April 28, 2002, depicts the surface fronts, surface dew points (dashed lines) and upper-level jet stream winds (solid lines).

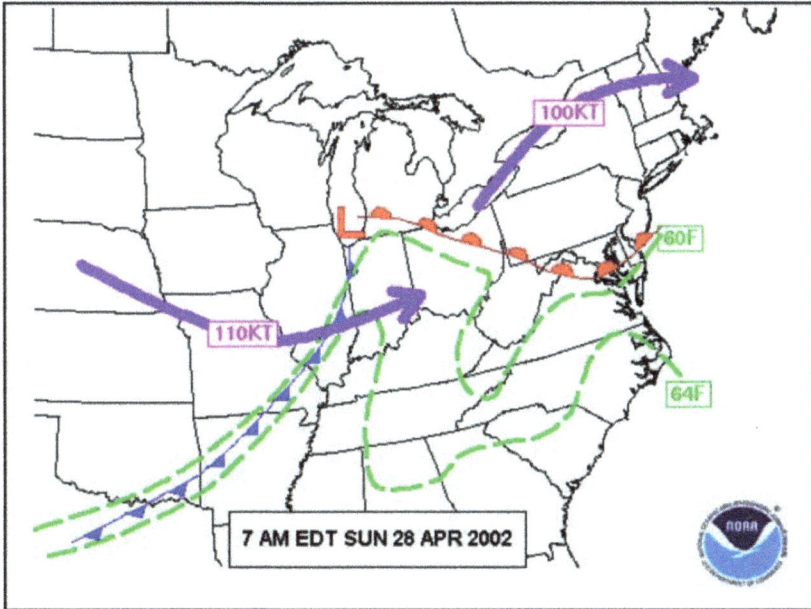

2-3: *Composite NOAA map for 7 a.m. on April 28, 2002.*

Cold Front

Warm Front

At 7 a.m. in the La Plata area, a warm front was located just south of the town. Cool air reinforced by clouds and precipitation led to a stable air mass early in the day. The dew point was 60 degrees Fahrenheit which was only moderately favorable for the development of widespread severe weather. You generally need dew points above 60 degrees to support widespread severe weather.

However, further west, weather conditions were deteriorating rapidly. Supercell thunderstorms developed during the late morning over

Kentucky along a strong cold front and in association with an upper-level system. Jet stream winds greater than 125 mph were associated with this upper-level system and contributed to an atmosphere conducive to the development of these supercell thunderstorms and tornadoes. Supercell thunderstorms are the most violent type of severe thunderstorm and produce large hail and damaging winds. They represent the majority of the tornadoes that occur across the United States.

A stunning photograph of the La Plata supercell was taken on April 28, 2002 in very early afternoon by William Rison, a passenger aboard an Eastern Airlines flight, probably near the Kentucky/West Virginia border.

2-4: *The La Plata supercell.*

An excellent description of the intricate mechanics of a supercell can be found at https://en.wikipedia.org/wiki/Supercell.

The supercell that would eventually develop into the F4 La Plata tornado was born around 1:00 p.m. along the border of Kentucky and West Virginia just south of Barboursville in Cabell County, West Virginia. The National Weather Service issued a tornado watch at 1:21 p.m. for most of

West Virginia and the western Maryland panhandle; at 3:05 p.m., another tornado watch was issued for most of western Virginia and most of Maryland. The first tornado warning was made for Virginia at 4:37 p.m.

The following image, adapted from Google Maps, shows the track and associated timeline of the La Plata cyclic supercell as it crossed West Virginia and Virginia up to the point when it entered Charles County in Southern Maryland where it once again became a tornado. The storm, at this point in time, had traveled approximately four-hundred miles in distance.

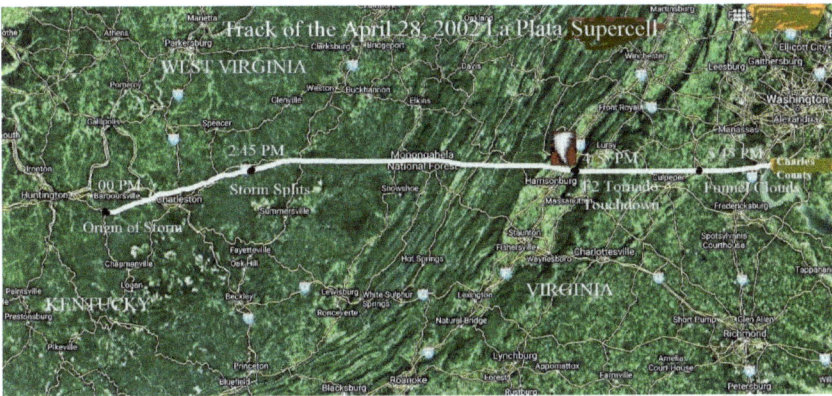

2-5: *Track of the La Plata supercell through West Virginia and Virginia.*

At approximately 2:45 p.m. on April 28, the supercell split northwest of Summersville, Virginia. Many supercells split, especially early in their lifetimes. The reasons for storm splits involve variations above the ground of wind speeds and shear within the storm's environment. In the northern hemisphere, left movers tend to spin clockwise (anticyclonic) and the right movers turn counterclockwise (cyclonic). The right split has access to stronger storm-relative inflow and shear, and last longer. The storm crossed the Appalachian Mountains between 3 p.m. and 4 p.m. Eastern Standard Time. Just like hurricanes, many tornadoes weaken as they cross mountains. However, the storm that struck La Plata remained a strong supercell as it crossed from West Virginia into Virginia. The supercell survived the split, retaining much of its strength and resiliency as it crossed the mountains.

2-6: The La Plata supercell splits.

The WFO (Weather Forecast Office) Baltimore/Washington issued its first tornado warning for Shenandoah County, Virginia at 4:37 p.m.

The cyclic supercell produced an F2 tornado in Shenandoah County, Virginia. The tornado is seen here crossing the northbound lane of I-81 at 5:01 p,m. It is now about two hours before the supercell would produce another tornado in western Charles County, Maryland.

2-7: The F2 tornado.

The tornado originally touched down east of Quicksburg, Virginia at 4:55 p.m. and would remain on the ground for four miles as shown on this image adapted from a 3-D Google Earth Map.

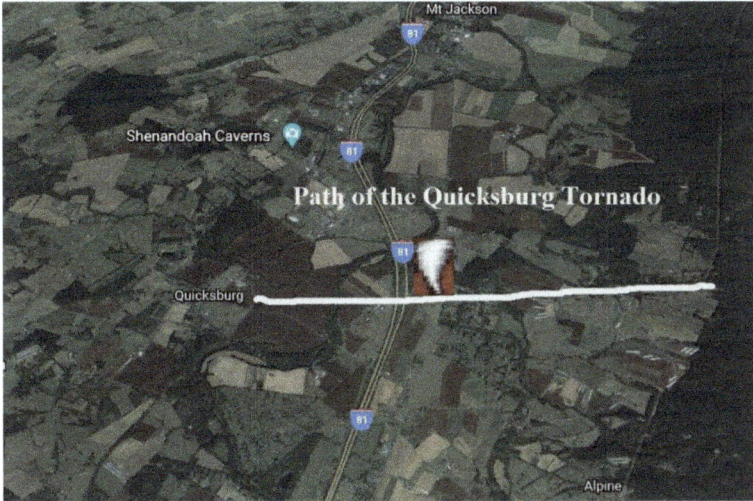

2-8: *Path of the F2 tornado.*

A detailed narration of the Quicksburg tornado mentions that a tractor-trailer was overturned as the storm crossed Interstate 81 and that considerable damage was done to the poultry industry in the area, as damaged cages led to freedom for a multitude of turkeys and chickens.

2-9: *Flying tractor-trailer.*

2-10: *Poultry on the run.*

Distance (miles)	Date	Magnitude	Start Lat/Log	End Lat/Log	Length	Width	Fatalities	Injuries	Property Damage	Crop Damage	Affected County
4.0	2002-04-28	2	38°41'N / 78°40'W	38°41'N / 78°35'W	4.00 Miles	75 Yards	0	2	1.6M	0	Shenandoah

Brief Description: A tornado injured 2 people, destroyed 4 homes, damaged 56 additional homes and 36 agricultural structures, downed numerous trees, and blew over a tractor-trailer on Interstate 81. A long-lived supercell thunderstorm formed over northwest Rockingham County during the afternoon of the 28th. This severe storm moved east at 45 MPH, damaging property all of the way to the Potomac River. This same storm later produced a devastating F4 tornado in La Plata, MD. While the storm moved through North Central Virginia, it produced an F2 tornado in Shenandoah County, a significant funnel cloud in Fauquier County, large hail, heavy downpours, and scattered wind damage. In Shenandoah County, an F2 tornado touched down just east of Quicksburg near the intersection of Quicksburg Road and Old Bridge Road. The tornado stayed on the ground for 4 miles before it dissipated while moving up the west side of Massanutten Mountain. The twister was estimated to be about 75 yards wide and it caused a total of $1.6 million in damage. Along the path of the tornado, three residential structures were destroyed, 12 structures were heavily damaged, and 15 had minor damage. Four poultry houses and 15 barns were destroyed. Five poultry houses, two silos, and a mile of fencing was also damaged. On Old Bridge Road, a silo and three barns were damaged. Airborne roof debris and high winds hit a tractor-trailer on I-81 and caused it to flip onto its side. The driver of the tractor-trailer was treated for minor injuries. The tornado moved across I-81 and Route 11 into the Kay Hill subdivision. Homes were damaged and trees were downed on Lower and Upper Forge Road. A mobile home on Mantz Drive was destroyed. The tornado moved east across Smith Creek to Smith Creek Road and Franwood Lane where it caused significant damage. A two-story home just off Smith Creek Road was severely damaged by debris from a neighbor's 60-foot-high grain silo. A woman inside the structure was treated for bruises. On Franwood Lane, two turkey houses were destroyed and four were severely damaged. One dog that lived on the property was killed and another was injured. A cat was never found. A shed was damaged and work equipment was scattered across the property. At Franwood Farms Airport, 5 people took shelter from the storm in a hangar. A person in the hangar said the walls kept coming closer together as the tornado approached and eventually the roof blew off the building. The tornado also flipped a plane on the landing strip. The tornado's path was visible up to two miles east of Franwood Farms through a path of damaged trees in the forest. The path of tree damage ended as the topography sloped up Massanutten Mountain into George Washington National Forest. In addition, an orchard west of Mt. Jackson just north of the tornado's path, sustained hail damage. In Rockingham County, dime sized hail fell in Bergton for ten minutes. In Page County, golf ball sized hail fell in Rileyville. Power lines were downed in Stanley. In Culpeper County, a tree was downed onto Route 522 near Route 633 in Norman. In Fauquier County, a funnel cloud was photographed by a meteorologist on a hill near Fauquier Springs. The time series of photos shows the funnel never reaching the ground. High winds downed a large tree and utility poles onto Harts Mill and Spriggs roads about 5 miles west of Warrenton. In New Baltimore, dime sized hail was reported. In Prince William County, quarter sized hail fell in Woodbridge and Manassas. Golf ball sized hail caused property damage in Dale City. A total of 2.20 inches of rain fell in Canova as the storm passed through.

2-11: *Quicksburg tornado narrative.*

The cyclic supercell that produced the Quicksburg tornado began to relinquish its tornadic signature while moving up the west side of the Massanutten Mountain Ridge, a segment of the Ridge and Valley Appalachians. Once it crossed the Ridge and Valley, Blue Ridge, and

Piedmont Mountains, the storm wouldn't produce another tornado until it struck western Charles County, Maryland.

2-12: *Approaching the Massanutten Mountain Ridge.*

Here is a 3-D Google Earth Map showing Mt. Jackson, Quicksburg and the Massanutten Mountain Ridge.

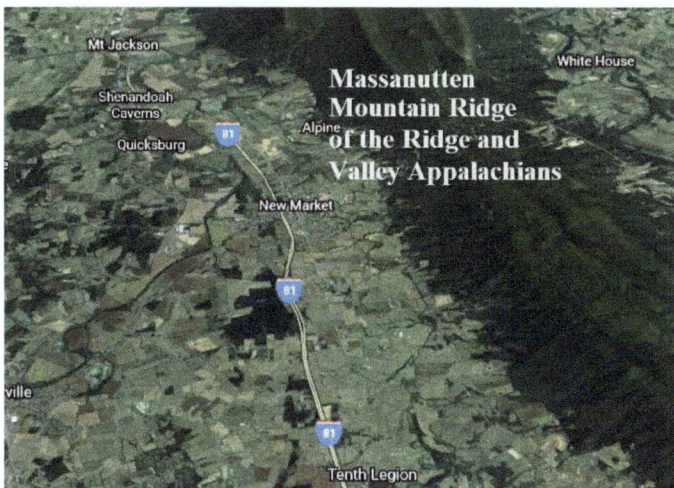

2-13: *The Massanutten Mountain Ridge.*

The storm continued its eastward trek beginning at 5:45 p.m. and continuing until 6:04 p.m. Doppler radar from the Sterling National Weather Service Forecast Office recorded four severe weather sightings over Fauquier County. Although this sequence of radar sightings showed the formation of a hook echo at 5:57 p.m., often associated with a supercell tornado, actual visual sightings during this period indicated that none of the funnel clouds, as witnessed by ground observers, actually developed into a tornado.

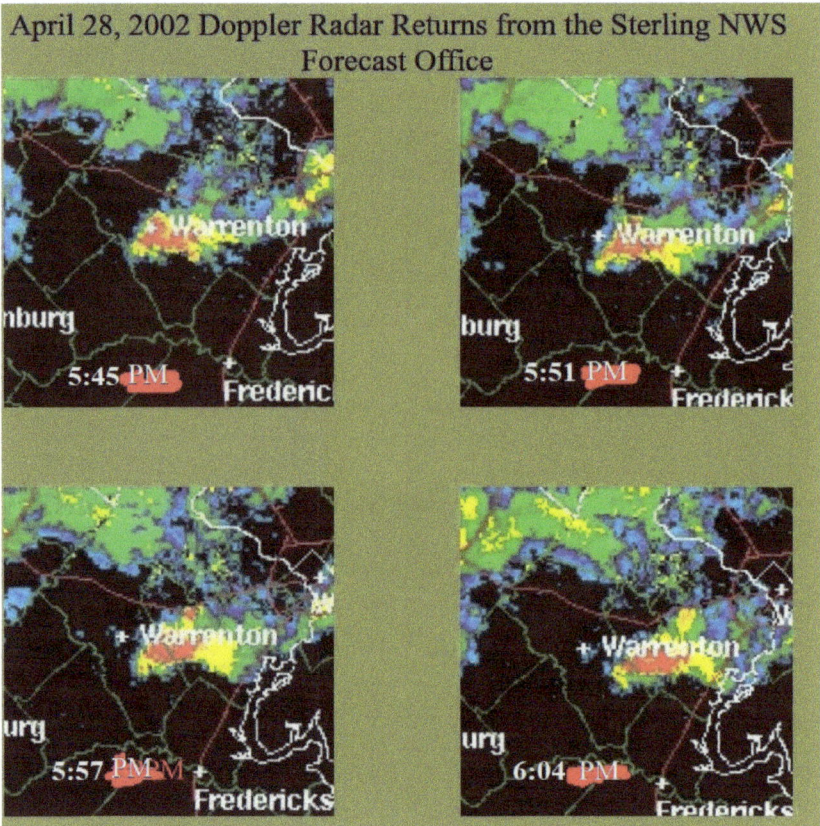

April 28, 2002 Doppler Radar Returns from the Sterling NWS Forecast Office

2-14: *Warrenton Doppler.*

See https://en.wikipedia.org/wiki/Hook_echo for an excellent description of a hook echo.

The National Weather Service may consider the presence of a hook echo coinciding with a tornado vortex signature as sufficient to justify issuing a tornado warning. Although tornado warnings were issued along the storm's path across northern Virginia through 6:45 p.m., no tornadoes actually occurred during this period.

Supercell thunderstorms developed funnel clouds near Opal, Virginia on April 28, 2002, approximately one hour before the supercell generated F3 and F4 tornado strikes in downtown La Plata. Mike Eckert, a meteorologist with the National Weather Service, took a picture of a funnel cloud over Fauquier County.

2-15: *Funnel cloud over Opal, Virginia.*

The storm moved across Page, Culpeper, Fauquier, and Prince William Counties, but produced little damage except for reports of hail.

CHAPTER 3

The Tornado's Path through Western Charles County

The meteorological dynamics of the storm changed dramatically as it crossed the Potomac River, beginning around 6:51 p.m. As reported in the article, **Born in Midwest, fueled by the Potomac** published in the Special Edition of the *Maryland Independent* for Wednesday, May 1, 2002, staff writer Jonathan D. Jones wrote: "as the killer storm crossed the Potomac River Sunday night, the already powerful upper-level system gained considerable strength from the atmospheric change along the river." He reported that Christopher Strong, a meteorologist with the National Weather Service observed that, "When it hit that small but important atmospheric boundary along the Potomac River, that's what really sent that storm into a tornadic super cell." Strong said, "It isn't uncommon for storms to intensify when crossing the Potomac."

According to the **Analysis of the April 28, 2002 La Plata, Maryland Tornado Mesoscale Environment** by Stephen J. Rogowski and Steven M. Zubrick, NOAA/National Weather Service Sterling, Virginia, "As the storm progressed further east across the Potomac River, it entered a core of developed low-level jet. The low-level jet is a common experience for forecasters in the Great Plains and Eastern United States. As the name implies, it is a fast moving ribbon of air in the low levels of the atmosphere. With substantially increased shear and cooling midlevel temperatures now providing moderate instability, the storm once again developed a hook echo at 2251 UTC (6:51 p.m.) over the Potomac River as rotation increased."

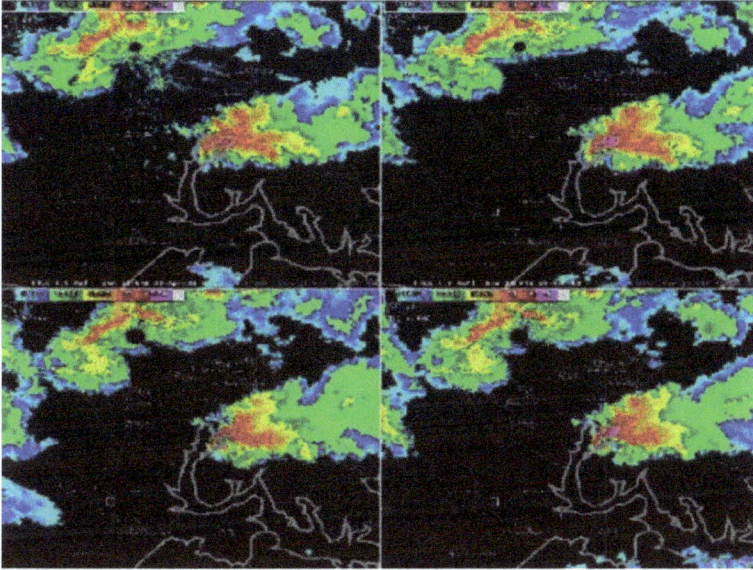

3-1: *Storm over the Potomac River.*

As the storm entered the Potomac River, Megan Lima, then residing at the Navy Offsite Housing in Woodbridge, Virginia, reported the following to me. "We saw a dark ugly storm crossing into the Potomac River. Suddenly, we were assailed by hail coming from the direction of the storm as it churned across the river." The following image, adapted from Google Maps, shows this passage over the Potomac River.

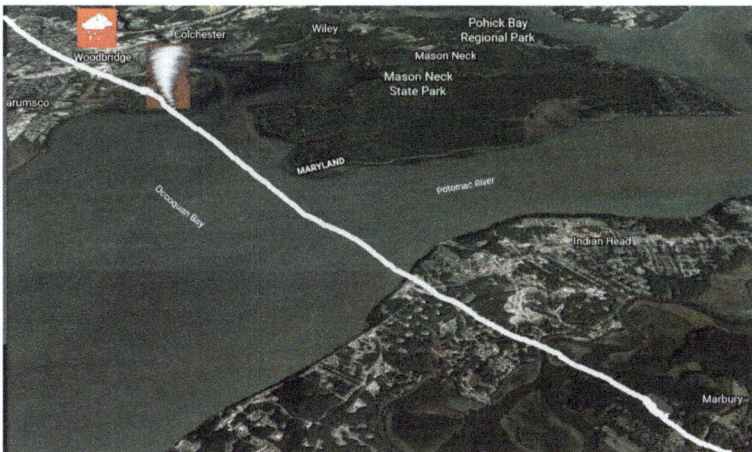

3-2: *Hail over Woodbridge.*

Before we proceed any further, let us examine the atmospheric conditions in southern Maryland, including the town of La Plata, shortly after the storm crossed the Potomac River and entered western Charles County.

Unfortunately for the inhabitants of this entire area, all of the ingredients needed for strong rotating thunderstorms were in place. A strong jet stream existed over the northeast with winds in the upper-atmosphere around 125 mph. A strong upper level trough provided atmospheric conditions favorable for the development of supercell thunderstorms and tornadoes. As the Washington, D.C. area sat in the middle of these two jet streams, we were in the prime place for rising motion giving a "coupled-jet structure." A cold front was west of Washington, D.C., ensuring more vertical motion for thunderstorm initiation and skies cleared in the morning hours leading up to the event, which allowed for maximum heating throughout the day. A dew point level of 64 degrees Fahrenheit existed for the entire state of Maryland, ideal for the formation of supercell thunderstorms and tornadoes.

A composite NOAA image from 7 p.m. EDT on April 28, 2002, depicted the surface fronts, surface dew points (dashed lines) and upper-level jet stream winds (solid lines).

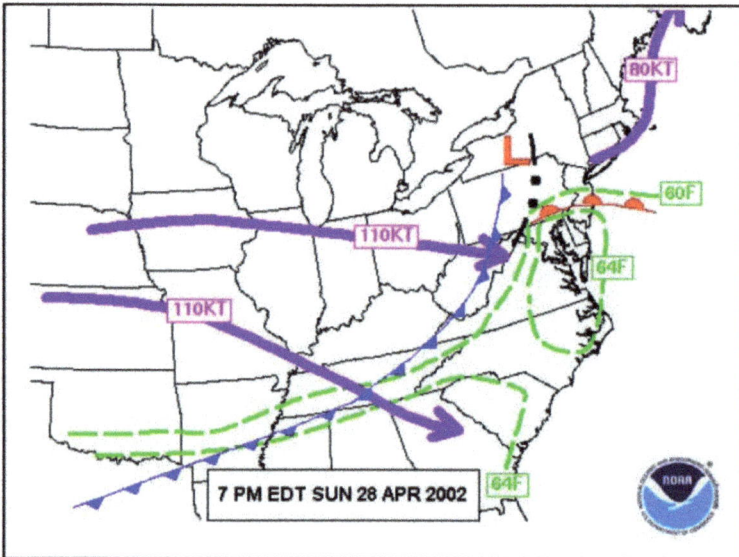

3-3: Composite NOAA map for 7 p.m. on April 28, 2002.

Cold Front

Warm Front

Without a confirmed tornado report (although a F2 tornado had actually hit south of Mt. Jackson, Virginia earlier in the day which was never reported to the forecasters), believing the supercell's tornadic potential was deceasing, and the unwillingness of the National Weather Service to "jump the gun" and declare a false tornado warning, the WFO Baltimore/ Washington forecasters issued only a severe thunderstorm warning for Extreme southern Anne Arundel, Prince George's, Calvert and northern Charles Counties in Maryland. The forecast stated, "Radar indicated a severe thunderstorm" at 1845 or 6:45p.m. They predicted the storm would go north of La Plata, closer to the Waldorf Town Center, which is about ten miles north of La Plata.

In actuality, the tornado made landfall at 6:56 p.m. south of Marbury in western Charles County in the Smallwood State Park. The F1 tornado developed about a mile east of the Mattawoman Creek and two miles east of the Potomac River.

3-4: Landfall near Marbury, Maryland.

Residents in the area experienced large hail, which damaged property and automobiles left outside. Kathryn and David Newman, living at 4162

Boykin Place, Indian Head, Maryland, had extensive hail damage to their cars as a result of the hailstorm. They live approximately seven miles from where the tornado made landfall, as seen in this image adapted from a 3-D Google Earth Map.

3-5: At home with the Newmans.

Hail covered the Newman property as well as the grounds of many other homeowners in western Charles County.

3-6: Hail in western Maryland.

The tornado would now begin its thirty-eight-mile trek through the southern Maryland counties of Charles and Calvert, where it had reached a maximum intensification of F4, before continuing through Dorchester County (F3) and Wicomico County (F0).

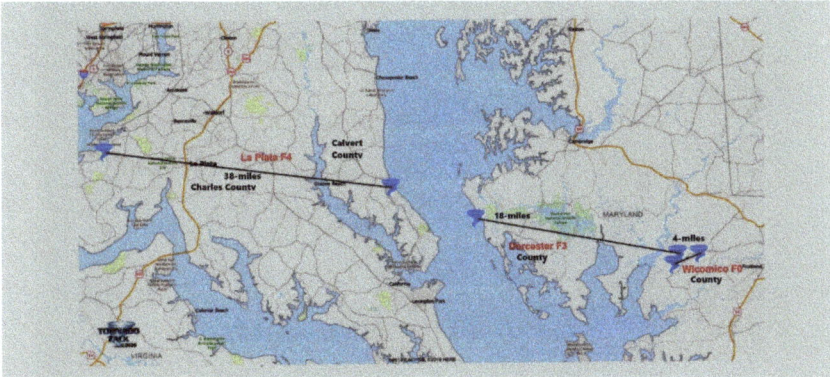

3-7: *Track of the La Plata tornado.*

The newly developed La Plata tornado now began its trek from Marbury, Maryland, moving in a southeast direction through western Charles County. The tornado continued on this track across Mason Spring Road about a half a mile north of Pisgah as seen in this image adapted from Google Maps. It was a F1 at this time (estimated maximum winds 75 to 112 mph). Its width was about 200 yards.

3-8: *Onward to Ripley.*

The tornado hit a residential community along Ripley Road just southwest of Ripley and tore the entire roof off a home. Damage in this vicinity was rated F2 (maximum winds estimated at over 113 mph). This diagram was provided courtesy of Tim Marshall at Haag Engineering.

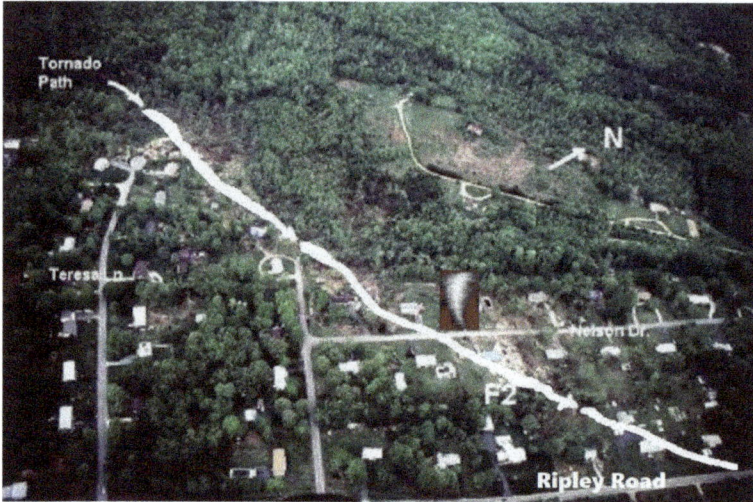

3-9: *Tornado along Ripley Road.*

Directly south of Ripley, at his home in the town of Welcome, Dr. George Wathen was preparing an outside barbeque. He mentioned to the author that he heard what he thought was a train in the distance, knowing full well that there weren't any train tracks nearby to account for the sound. This image, adapted from Google Maps, shows the location of Welcome, Maryland, relative to the path taken by the tornado.

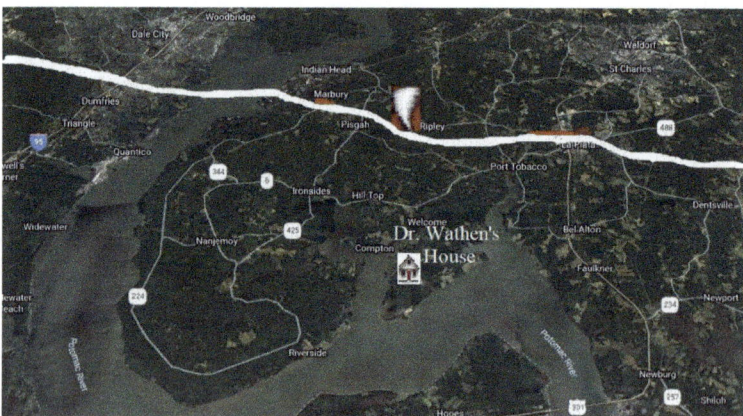

3-10: *Sound of a train in the distance.*

The tornado continued southeast, where it maintained its F1 intensity until it neared Rose Hill Road. At this location, the tornado appeared to strength to F2 intensity based on the extensive tree and structural damage observed on the ground.

At Hill Spring Drive, about a mile and a half west of La Plata, some F3 damage occurred (maximum winds estimated at over 158 mph). The width of the tornado also increased to about 330 yards wide. This adapted 3-D Google Earth Map shows the tornado's path.

3-11: *Hill Spring Drive.*

Rose Hill Road connects to Marshall Corner Road as it crosses Hawthorne Road (Route 225). Situated on Marshall Corner Road is the Town of Pomfret, as shown in this adapted image from Google Maps.

3-12: *Town of Pomfret.*

The following photograph, taken by Eric Beach, shows some of the remarkable baseball-sized hail stones (2.75 inches) that pummeled the community of Pomfret, Maryland, as the tornado continued to move from west to east. Note the protuberances on the stones. This is evidence that they were subjected to a series of strong updrafts, which enabled them to increase in size each time they passed through layers of super-cooled water droplets. Eventually, they were too large to be supported by the storm's updraft. Hail greater than ¾ inch (1.9 cm) in diameter (size of a penny) is a criterion for a severe thunderstorm, according to the National Weather Service.

3-13: *Hailstones at Pomfret*.

Between Hill Spring Drive, along Morgans Ridge Road, and onward to Quailwood, the tornado severely damaged numerous homes with F2 and F3 force wind intensities. The image has been modified from a photograph submitted to the Charles County Government by Warren Robinette.

3-14: *Along Morgans Ridge Road.*

As it approached the Quailwood Subdivision, the foreboding sky foretold the destruction which was to come within minutes.

3-15: *Tornado approaches Quailwood.*

After crossing West Quail Lane and Quail Court, within the Quailwood Subdivision, the tornado, as shown in this image adapted from a 3-D Google Earth Map, traveled in the same southeasterly direction, destroying much of the Archbishop Neale School with winds of F3 intensity based on the actual observed damage seen by the National Weather Service survey assessment team. The tornado's course would next threaten the Town of La Plata itself.

3-16: *Through Quailwood.*

CHAPTER 4

The Tornado Arrives in La Plata

Minutes after making landfall in Marbury, the now F3 tornado arrived at the outskirts of La Plata. The fast-moving 58 mile per hour storm traveled the nine miles from Marbury to the outskirts of the town in four minutes, and to the heart of the town in six minutes.

This GOES 8 satellite photograph shows the La Plata tornado as a large dimple right under the "Maryland" label. The time of this photograph was 7:02 p.m. EST.

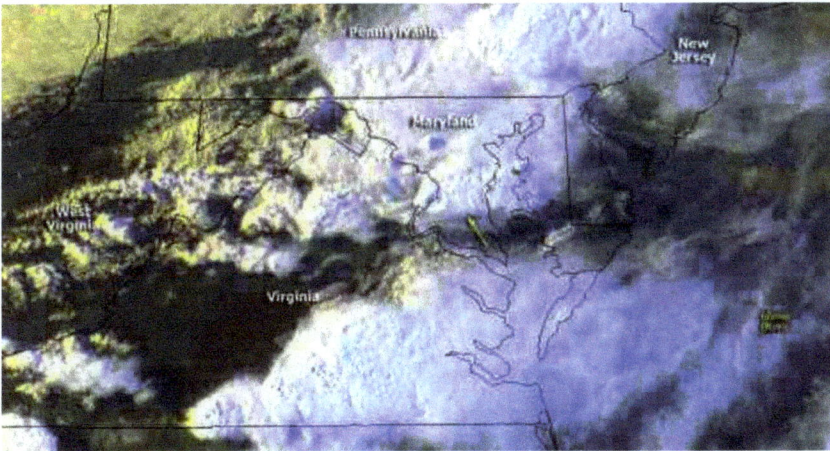

4-1: GOES 8 La Plata tornado.

The tornado is visibly seen at 7:00 p.m. from a vantage point at St. Mary's Avenue and Frederick Drive southwest of the town, only minutes before striking downtown La Plata.

4-2: Tornado looking from St. Mary's Avenue in La Plata.

The author lives at 9160 Preference Drive, in Preference Estates, which is about four miles south of the Town of La Plata. On the night of April 28, 2002, my family and I were watching the great BBC mini-series **I Claudis** starring Derek Jacobi. The series is a fascinating behind the scenes story of the various Emperors of the early Roman Empire, told from the perspective of the elderly Emperor Claudis who narrates each episode of the series. Claudius' grandmother, Livia, was in the process of poisoning someone when at around 7 p.m., our lights flickered but did not go out. I looked out my front window, in a northwesterly direction, and saw the sky was exhibiting a dirty, darkish gray, sickly hue. I heard nothing, as the television was probably a bit loud. Since I was not watching a standard network station, I didn't see any watches or warning flashed on the television screen, alerting me to any danger. In fact, it wouldn't be until the next morning that I learned of the tragedy that had struck downtown La Plata. I was stopped by a State Trooper at the intersection of Routes 301 and 6 around 6:00 a.m. I was allowed through after telling him that I worked for the Department of Energy in the Office of Emergency Management. Debris filled the air as if I was in a dense fog. I got as far as Martin's gas station on Charles Street and turned around as the ground was covered by downed electrical wires. I continued driving to work in Washington, D.C. via Hawthorne Road (Route 228) and Indian Head Highway (Route

210). The following image adapted from Google Maps shows the location of my house relative to the path of the tornado.

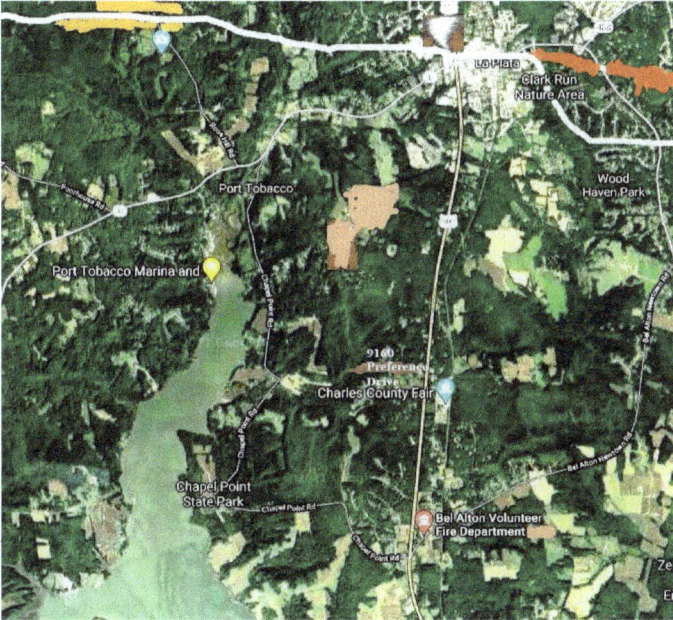

4-3: **9160 Preference Drive.**

I received the following testimony from Jody Nyers, who once lived in the Town of Bel Alton, which is about two miles further south of my home off Route 301.

We lived in Bel Alton and on that evening (April 28, 2002) my daughters were outside with the neighborhood kids and I was doing some laundry. My husband was the Fire Chief of Bel Alton Volunteer Fire Department and we had a scanner/pager on our counter. While standing in the laundry room, the scanner went off (wildly) and it immediately caught my attention, so I listened to the 911 dispatchers saying something about a possible tornado in the La Plata area. At that time, my husband ran out the door and jumped into his Chief's car and headed to the firehouse. Also, my neighbors called me and screamed into the phone "Get all the kids into the basement NOW! There's a tornado heading our way."

Of course, this happened so quickly, and we had no idea where the tornado was heading but I called all the kids into the house and we all went to the basement while listening to the scanner. Needless to say, time stood still for a while. The neighbors pulled into my driveway shortly after they called and indicated they witnessed the tornado coming over several neighborhoods in La Plata, above Arch Bishop Neale Catholic School and the shopping center at the intersection of Rt. 301 and Rt. 6. We stayed in the basement for about an hour watching TV for updates.

When we got the all-clear (in Bel Alton), the neighbors went home, and I went over to the firehouse to see if I could help. That led to hours of volunteering making food and delivering it to those working on and around the scene. This was done under the cover of darkness due to power outages and nighttime setting in.

4-4: **Jody's Story**

This image, adapted from Google Maps, shows the location of the La Plata Village Center relative to the location of the tornado as it approached the intersection of Routes 301 and 6 before entering the heart of the business district in downtown La Plata.

4-5: *The La Plata Village Center.*

This photograph was taken by Tom Albrittain from the vantage point of the La Plata Village Center, as the tornado approached the intersection of Routes 301 and 6, perhaps in the vicinity of the Archbishop Neale School and the United Methodist Church.

4-6: View of tornado from the La Plata Village Center.

On April 28, 2002, Joseph and Judy Thomason made a video of the La Plata tornado as they traveled south on Route 301, driving towards La Plata. The video begins as the Thomasons' car approaches and intersects with Washington Avenue (branching off to the left) and Turkey Hill Road (branching off to the right). They continued south on 301 for another three miles until they reached the La Plata Village Center and the Food Lion grocery store, a distance of approximately three miles and three minutes of travel time, as measured by the author. During this period of time, the video shows the tornado approaching and then crossing the intersection of Routes 301 and 6. The video appears to show the tornado between 7:02 p.m. and 7:05 p.m. on that fateful night. The following still from the video, looking in a southeasterly direction from the La Plata Village Center, shows that the tornado has reached the heart of the La Plata business district. This film is included in a video produced by Dr. William T. Hark entitled *Eastern Fury*, Tornadoes of the Eastern United States.

4-7: Tornado as seen from the Food Lion.

The following article appeared in the Special Edition of the *Maryland Independent* on May 1, 2002. Johnny Boy's is not far from where the photograph of the tornado was taken, on St. Mary's Avenue, which is shown next.

> *'A funnel, twisting the sky down'*
>
> *Former Maryland Independent news editor Jim Brocker and his wife, Conni James, came through La Plata minutes after the tornado touched down on April 28. This is their account.*
>
> *"At 7 p.m. Sunday, we were eating beef sandwiches at Johnny Boy's, watching the black clouds of a weather front swallow a beautiful blue sky. Pulling out of the parking lot, we debated whether to go to WaWa for decaf and dessert, or go home and duck the storm. As we pulled out of our parking space, we noticed other customers' outstretched arms were pointing north, and as our gaze followed, we saw it: a large funnel, twisting the sky down toward the trees, veering diagonally across our path.*

In a few seconds, it was past. We were unnerved, but unhurt, so we headed north on U.S. 301 for coffee. As we approached La Plata, traffic began to slow, and we began to notice damage... The motel (Deluxe Inn Motel) to our left was damaged. Debris blocked Centennial Street. Burger King was blown out, True Value Hardware was crushed, a waterfall from a broken main flowing through the rubble. We sat stunned as the scene unfolded. People were walking, dazed and hushed. In the stillness, one woman ran screaming toward the damaged motel. People tried to stop her, ask her if she was okay, but she just kept on running and screaming."

The following eyewitness account of the tornado was presented in a book entitled The Path of Destruction – La Plata, Maryland – April 28, 2002, generously loaned to me by Mr. William Daniel Mayer, the former County Commissioner for District 1 (La Plata).

Cynthia Kercher's Tornado Story

At 7:00 on April 28th, I was traveling west on Route 6 through La Plata, heading for home in Port Tobacco. In the car with me were my 6-year old son Dillon, my 14-year old daughter Rebecca and her best friend Erica. As we passed Christ Episcopal Church and headed down the hill towards the light at Route 301, I saw something out of the corner of my eye and asked the girls what it was. Erica and Rebecca both yelled, "It's spinning!" As I came to a stop at the light, we all looked straight ahead and a huge gray funnel shot down out of the clouds. I felt like I was looking at Death, and my son burst in to tears and shouted, "I'm too young to die." Rebecca and Erica both exclaimed, "Oh cool, a tornado!" Fortunately, I was able to back up because the car behind me had left about 20 feet. I threw the car into reverse, turned right across the median and up into the Exxon parking lot on the corner. I put the car in park (as it turned out I never even turned the car off), grabbed Dillon and yelled for the girls to follow me and ran into the Tiger Mart. We ran into a back storeroom and got on the floor against a wall. Thirty seconds later, the tornado hit the Tiger Mart. I would estimate it was only one minute after I had first seen the tornado. The four of us held onto each other chanting "God is great, God is good, God is great, God is good." The tornado destroyed most of the Tiger Mart, but the room we were in wasn't damaged and we escaped without a scratch. My car was picked up, smashed, and thrown into the car wash behind the mart. We were very fortunate that day to have escaped without any injuries.

Since the 28th, many people asking about our experience want to know what it sounded like. The four of us heard our prayers more loudly than we heard the tornado and that is the sound that I remember the most. I know that our faith has helped us to recover from the traumatic effects of living through an F-4 tornado.

4-8: Kercher's Story

The following image, adapted from Google Maps, shows the various routes taken by our story tellers on the day of the tornado.

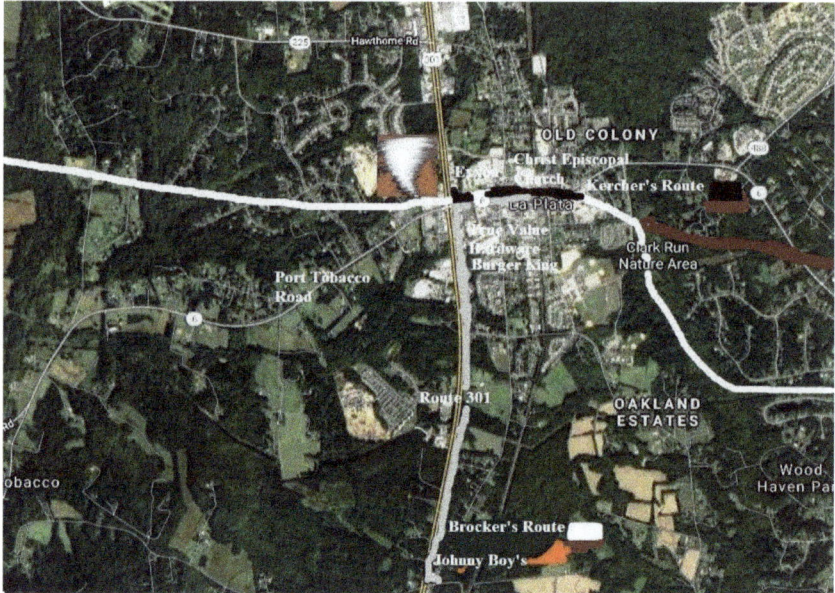

4-9: Routes taken.

1900-1903 (7:00 p.m. – 7:03 p.m.) **Forecaster calls Charles County, Maryland 911 center and warns them of a tornado. The forecaster received immediate feedback from 911 operator of a tornado in La Plata at the time.**

1902 (7:02 p.m.) **Southern Prince George's, Calvert, Charles, extreme northern St. Mary's Counties in Maryland.**

"RADAR indicated a tornado."

This photograph was taken by Jeff Posey from behind his pickup truck. The photographer was on South Maple Avenue behind the Chapman and Bowling Building, looking northeast. In that instant, the old water tower was in view, just before being toppled by the approaching storm. At the time, Posey was transporting his Cub Cadet mower, which he still owes.

4-10: *Tornado as seen from South Maple Avenue.*

This NOAA Geostationary Operational Environmental Satellite (GOES) 8 image was taken at 23:02 UTC (7:02 p.m.) and shows the circular outline of the tornado over La Plata.

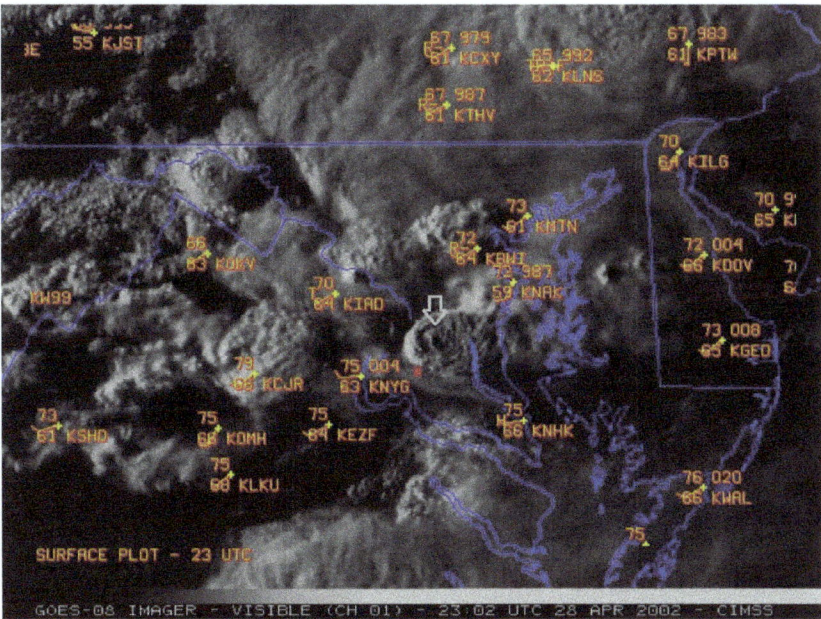

4-11: *NOAA satellite image of tornado over La Plata.*

Live Doppler Radar, aired on WJLA Channel 7 (Washington, D.C.), clearly shows the typical Hook Echo associated with this tornado crossing Maryland Routes 6 and 301 in La Plata at 7:04 p.m.

4-12: *Live Doppler Radar of La Plata tornado.*

Perhaps the most riveting and infamous photograph captured during the tornado was the one taken by Richard W. King, Jr. It appeared on the cover of the SPECIAL EDITION issue of the *Maryland Independent* dated Wednesday, May 1, 2002. The photograph was taken from the then Safeway parking lot, within the La Plata Shopping Center, looking towards Route 6 (Port Tobacco Road). The tornado is seen striking the La Plata United Methodist Church.

4-13: *Tornado in the La Plata Shopping Center.*

Within the structure of the tornado itself, the intensity of the wind varied from a F2 to a F4, depending on its exact location during its passage through town. Damage and eyewitness accounts indicate a second weaker tornado formed a quarter of a mile south of the first tornado.

4-14: *Two tornadoes in one.*

Both tornadoes crossed the heart of La Plata between 7:02 p.m. and 7:07 p.m., causing widespread F2 to F3 damage. Destruction in a one-square-block area on the east side of La Plata was most severe and rated F4. The secondary tornado would continue at least through Hawkins Gate Road, but would eventually dissipate. Meantime, the main tornado would continue moving east through the rest of Charles County, and into Calvert County and Dorchester County before finally dissipating in Wicomico County.

4-15: *Two vortexes.*

This satellite-generated map shows the path of the tornado as it passed through La Plata.

4-16: *Path of tornado through La Plata.*

In the Star Memorial Garden, in Downtown La Plata, red bricks have been laid in the exact direction the tornado took as it crossed the intersection of Routes 6 and 301. This would be the area where the tornado reached its maximum F4 intensity and ultimate destructive power. At this point, it begins its turn towards the Mitchell Supply Company on St. Mary's Avenue, bringing with it the tornado's most destructive winds.

4-17: Brick path of tornado's track.

The following two stills were captured from a film taken by Mike Abell. Again, the film is part of the Eastern Fury video. Abell's film was taken from a vantage point of an apartment complex on Caroline Drive off Washington Avenue in La Plata, looking southwest towards Downtown La Plata. It is about a quarter-mile north of Charles Street and the Court House. In the film, the tornado eventually moves in a southeasterly direction, away from Mr. Abell's location, allowing him to open his sliding door and get a better view of the tornado. When I talked to Mr. Abell, he advised me that the video time-stamp, appearing in his footage, was not correct. Note the flying debris field seen in the second still.

4-18: *Abell One.*

4-19: *Abell Two.*

This photograph was taken northeast of Mitchell's Supply near the intersection of Charles Street (Route 6) and Kent Avenue as the store was being destroyed.

4-20: Destruction of Mitchell's Supply store.

As the tornado moved east of the downtown area of La Plata, it left two dead, hundreds injured and property damage of approximately $100 million. A total of one hundred ninety-four businesses were damaged or destroyed, but the destruction was not over.

After leaving downtown La Plata, the tornado ripped through Clarks Run, crossed Route 6 (Charles Street) and Ellenwood Road, and moved towards Hawkins Gate Road as seen in this product of Google Maps.

4-21: *Tornado moves towards Hawkins Gate Road.*

At 516 Clarks Run Road in La Plata, Matt Ament made a home movie of the passing tornado moving from the southeast to due east as it passed in front of his home. The following is a still from this home movie. It is highly likely that Matt actually witnessed the passing of the weaker secondary tornado rather than the main tornado.

4-22: *At Clarks Run Road.*

During the actual filming itself, large hail began to fall.

4-23: *Hail at Clarks Run Road.*

The rather flamboyant and carefree demeanor expressed in this home video was the result of the participants probably not knowing of the horrible damage and human suffering which the tornado had already caused in Downtown La Plata. In these areas, homes were severely damaged, including some that were blown clear off their concrete foundations. One of the fatalities, William G. Erickson, fifty-one, was killed when his unfinished house on Hawkins Gate Road collapsed on top of him.

CHAPTER 5

The Tornado Continues Its Eastward Trek of Destruction

Although much of the area east of La Plata was rural, still one hundred homes, forty-nine businesses, and numerous barns were destroyed. Acres of dense forest were leveled. Damage to heavily wooded area, as well as a classic convergent and cyclonic pattern to how the trees fell, was captured in this photograph submitted to Charles County Government by Warren Robinette.

5-1: *Dense forests leveled.*

At 7:30 p.m., the tornado crossed into Calvert County where it killed an elderly couple, destroyed an additional ten homes, and damaged another one hundred twenty-five homes. It moved out onto the Chesapeake Bay just north of the Calvert Cliffs Nuclear Power Plant.

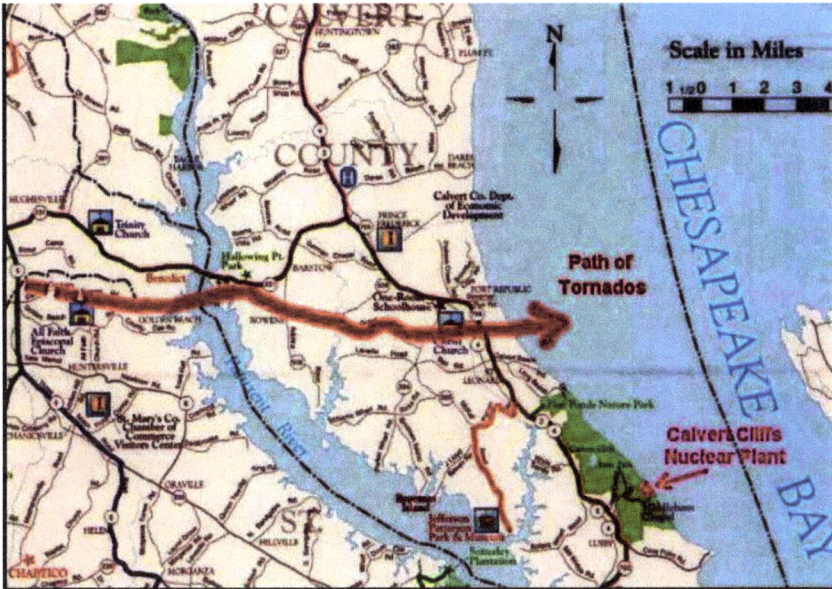

5-2: *Tornado at the Calvert Cliffs Nuclear Power Plant.*

A secondary vortex, a waterspout, formed for a few miles on the Bay. The primary tornado continued across Dorchester County, again intensifying to F3 before dissipating as it approached Salisbury in Wicomico County. The following image, adapted from a 3-D Google Earth Map, shows the path of the tornado from La Plata to near Salisbury.

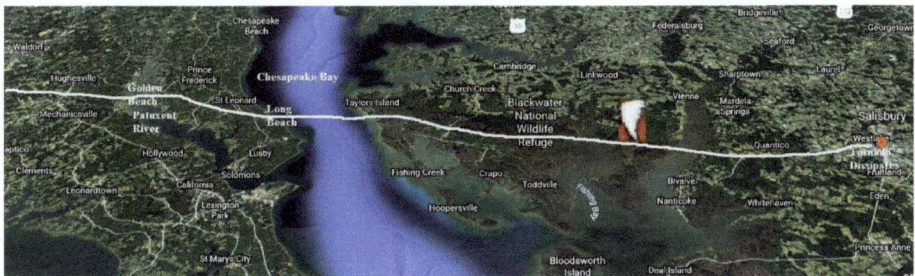

5-3: *Tornado path to near Salisbury.*

The following two photographs were obtained from a home video film taken by Andrew Gardner. Speaking to former WUSA 9 reporter Dave Statter, regarding the tornado as it appeared as a waterspout and then as it once again made landfall in Calvert County, Maryland, the filming was done from the vantage point of Route 4 across from the Flag Ponds Nature Park as seen in this product of Google Maps.

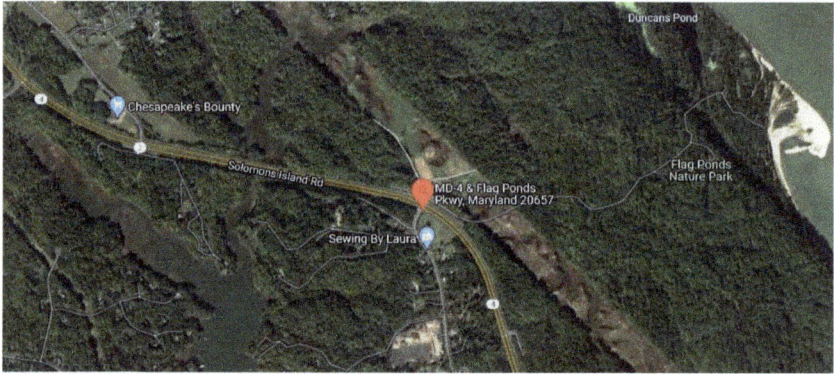

5-4: *Tornado in Calvert County.*

See: https://www.youtube.com/watch?v=e4k3IB_VcZc

The following sequence of stills taken from Andrew Gardner's video shows the tornado slowing, dropping out of the tornadic waterspout, and finally touching ground in the last two sequences of the stills.

5-5: *Tornadic waterspout starting to drop a tornado.*

5-6: Tornadic waterspout still dropping a tornado.

5-7: The tornado's intial landfall.

5-8: *Tornado moving on ground.*

Before leaving Calvert County for Dorcester County, the tornado put on a spectacular live-action show as it crossed into the Chesapeake Bay, just north of the Calvert Cliffs Nuclear Power Plant.

The following picture was taken by Ted L. Dutcher from Long Beach. He was a long-time resident of the town and walked across the street from his home in time to take the photograph of the tornado as it moved into the Chesapeake Bay as a waterspout.

5-9: *The Tornado moves into the Chesapeake Bay.*

A brilliant flash of lighting is seen close to the waterspout. It was taken by personnel at the Calvert Cliffs Nuclear Power Plant, who most likely stood in awe at what they were viewing, thankfully at a safe distance for them and the plant.

5-10: View from the Calvert Cliffs Nuclear Power Plant.

As the tornadic waterspout crossed the Chesapeake Bay, it occluded and a new waterspout formed.

5-11: Tornadic waterspouts.

This new tornadic waterspout crossed the Chesapeake Bay from Calvert County and began to approach Dorchester County. This crossing was captured in footage taken by John Cutter from the vantage point of his home at 3876 Punch Island Road on Taylors Island., as seen in this product from Google Maps.

5-12: *The Cutter home on Taylors Island.*

John Cutter notices a new waterspout at 7:41 p.m. to the left of the original waterspout. There are now two powerful tornadic waterspouts at the same time.

5-13: *Taylor Island view at 7:41 p.m..*

The second waterspout, now appearing more intense, passes in front of the weakening original waterspout by 7:43 p.m. The original waterspout dissipated by approximately 7:44 p.m. The second waterspout, now the sole tornadic waterspout, continues its approach to the coast. The tape ends at 7:46 p.m.

5-14: *Taylor Island view at 7:46 p.m.*

The tornadic waterspout made landfall in Dorchester County, south of Taylors Island, at approximately 8:02 p.m. as an F1 tornado, however, it quickly increased in intensity reaching a peak rating as an F3. Fortunately, the tornado traveled mostly through rural areas of the county; however, its intensity was still capable of downing a number of trees and flattening any homes or farms in its path. A video of the tornadic waterspout was filmed by Thomas (Tommy) Willey who, at the time, lived in Cambridge, Maryland. On April 28, 2002, he was traveling southwest on Route 16 in a truck, driven by his brother Kyle Willey, heading towards Taylors Island. They first saw and acknowledged the tornadic waterspout in the Chesapeake Bay at 7:49 p.m. At that exact point in time, they smartly recognized the approaching threat and began heading back home to Cambridge via Route 16. They captured this image of the tornadic waterspout, still in the Chesapeake Bay, at 7:57 p.m. just before the filming ends.

5-15: *Tornadic waterspout approaches Dorchester County.*

After leaving Dorchester County, the tornado weakened to an F0 eventually dissipating as it approached Salisbury, Maryland in Wicomico County at around 8:30 p.m., ninety-four minutes after it made landfall in western Charles County.

5-16: *Tornado weakens.*

CHAPTER 6
The Haunting Portraits of Destruction and Whirlwind Stories

The tornado caused in excess of $100 million dollars in property damage, destroying eight hundred sixty residential homes and one hundred ninety-four businesses in its wake. This chapter presents just some of damage caused to both residential and business properties on that fateful day in April of 2002.

The then F2 La Plata tornado, while crossing the sixty-three hundred to sixty-four hundred block of Nelson Drive, near Ripley, ripped the entire roof off of a house. This modified aerial photograph was provided courtesy of Tim Marshall at Haag Engineering.

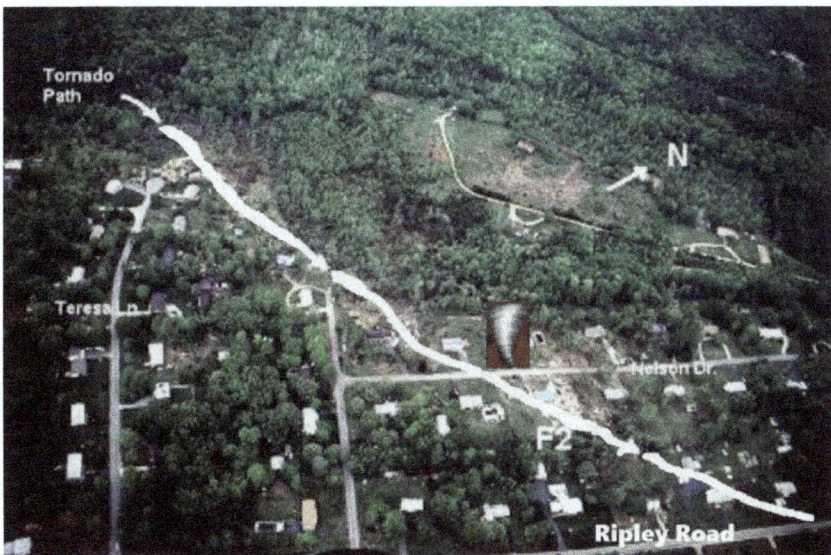

6-1: Damage on Nelson Drive.

The tornado continued its southeast path and incurred both F3 and F1 damage to these two residential homes on Hill Spring Drive. Again, this modified aerial photograph was provided courtesy of Tim Marshall.

6-2: *Damage on Hill Spring Drive.*

A number of residential homes were destroyed by F3 force winds along Morgans Ridge Road. The modified aerial photograph was again provided courtesy of Tim Marshall.

6-3: *Aerial of the damage along Morgans Ridge Road.*

Several homes were destroyed on Morgans Ridge Road and Quail Lane with some of these homes literally sliding off their foundation with the passage of the tornado. This particular house, on Morgans Ridge Road, slid off its foundation in a northerly direction, as captured in a photograph taken by Barbara Watson with NOAA/NWS.

6-4: *House damaged on Morgans Ridge Road.*

This damaged house on West Quail Lane seems to have a sofa as its sole property survivor. This poignant image was captured by Barbara Watson.

6-5: *House destroyed on West Quail Lane.*

The tornado swept through Quailwood crossing Bobwhite Court as seen in this modified aerial photograph provided by Tim Marshall. Several poorly attached homes slid off their foundation when hit by winds rated F1. However, those homes that lost their roof were attributed to F3 force winds.

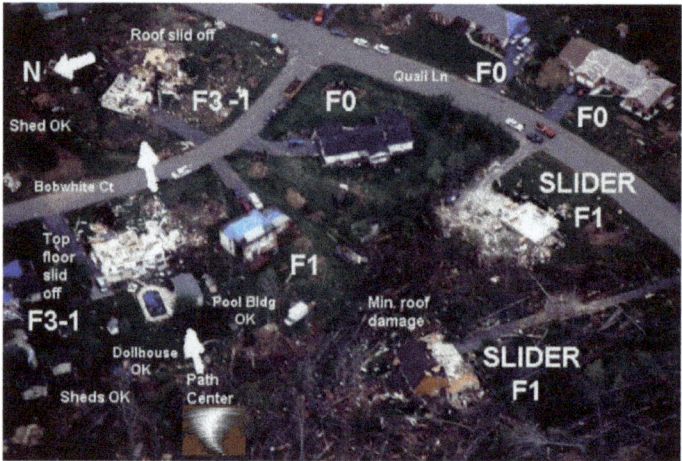

6-6: Sliders in Quailwood.

The following photograph, taken by Barbara Watson, shows a house which has lost its roof on Bobwhite Court in Quailwood.

6-7: House damage on Bobwhite Court.

Aerial and ground views of a house in Quailwood, apparently struck by F3 force winds, were captured in these photographs submitted to the Charles County Government by Warren Robinette.

6-8: Aerial view of Quailwood house damage.

6-9: Ground view of Quailwood house damage.

A first-hand account of what was happening in Quailwood was related to Victoria Weiss in September 2008, by Trish Kummerer in the publication, A WHIRLWIND OF STORIES, La Plata Tornado, 2002.

A Move We'll Never Forget

That Sunday we started packing first thing in the morning because we were supposed to be moving. We were going to sign our release on Monday and then we were going to move right after that. There was no TV or radio on. We had been packing all day long. Around late afternoon we had to come over to the house we were going to be moving into on Prince Charles Drive, for a walk-through. The walk-through went well so we left the house and headed to Hunan Star for dinner. I was driving and I noticed that the sky looked weird up in Waldorf. My husband and as we were getting into the car I said that the weather didn't look good in Waldorf. We currently lived in Quailwood so it took us three minutes to get home. My daughter wanted to go play for a little bit because she had been packing all day so she went out into the front yard. There were two girls that lived near us that were friends with my daughter. I told my husband that I was going to watch some TV. I turned it on and it turned right off. I turned it on again, it stayed on for about two seconds, you could hear the remote. I turned it back on and it stayed on for about two minutes. I was sitting on the coach in our living room near the sliding glass door and I could hear all this noise outside. I thought that was weird so I turned off the TV. I moved the curtain and all I saw was stuff flying by the window. The only thing I could think of was that my daughter was outside.

I got outside before my husband but my husband knew what that noise was because he grew up around tornadoes as a kid. I couldn't find my daughter and my husband was yelling at me to get back in the house because he knew what was coming. I had no idea; I thought there was a bad storm coming. My husband ran next door to look for my daughter. Because we had been packing, we had a trailer sitting at the end of the driveway. This trailer started coming at me and it stopped about an inch before it hit the garage. I was trying to get back into the house through the garage door but I couldn't get in. I had my whole body against the door, pushing it and I still couldn't get in. I knew it wasn't locked and all of a sudden, the next thing I know, I'm lying on the floor inside the house. I noticed later in the house that partway down the hallway there is an attic door and that was on the floor. My husband said that that must have released some pressure in the house, which is why I was able to get into the house.

We found out later that my next door neighbor knew the tornado was coming so she took all the kids in the basement so my daughter was ok. We had hail damage. The house behind us had a piece of someone's house go through their house; we have no idea where that came from.

6-10: Trish's Story

The home of Bonnie and Bruce Rafer is located at 6160 Weather View Place. Their home was struck by F2 force winds as the tornado passed through Quailwood to their north. The following image, adapted from Google Maps, shows the path of the tornado through Quailwood.

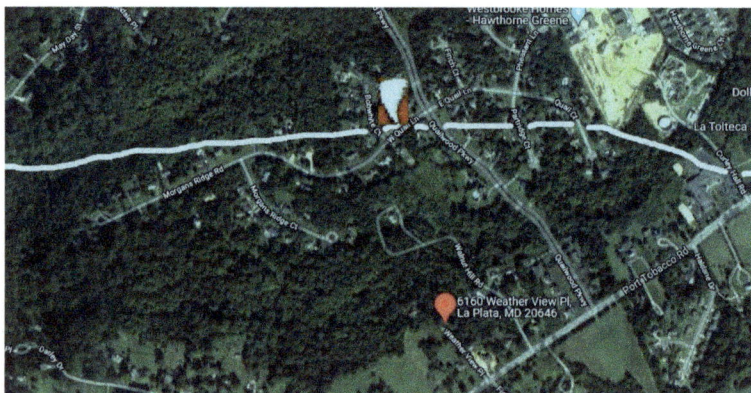

6-11: The location of the Rafer's home.

One of their double tulip polar trees sliced right through the Rafer house.

6-12: *Damage at the Rafer home.*

They related their firsthand experiences in the publication, The Path of Destruction – La Plata, Maryland - April 28, 2002.

6-13: *The Rafer's story.*

The following map shows the damage attributed to the 2002 La Plata tornado. I will reference this map in the pages to come. It appeared in the

Southern Maryland Extra edition of Sunday, June 16, 2002. The abbreviation LPTD will be used as an abbreviation for La Plata's Tornado Damage.

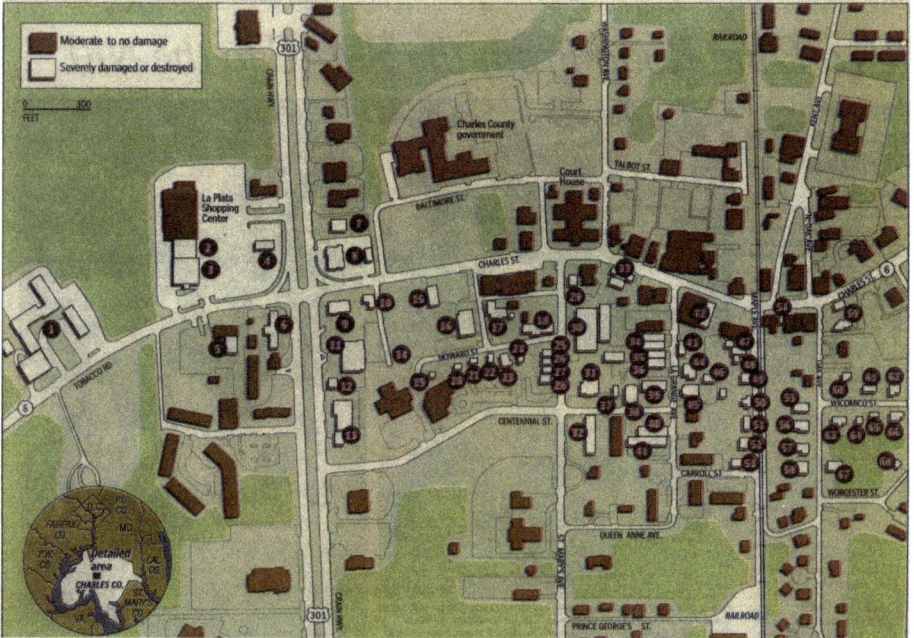

6-14: *La Plata's tornado damage.*

In the weeks since the April 28 tornado struck Southern Maryland, La Plata town officials and property owners have been taking stock of the damage and destruction.

The map above, based on one of several prepared for the town by Michael J. Pellegrino of PAS, a La Plata architecture and planning firm, shows the structures in the La Plata town center that were severely damaged or destroyed, according to local officials.

Beginning in July, as rebuilding plans take shape and projects get underway, *Southern Maryland Extra* will publish a monthly map showing what is being proposed and approved in the recovery effort in La Plata.

The tornado-damaged structures numbered on today's map are:

1. Archbishop Neale School
2. Shopping center: flower shop, dry cleaners, carryout Chinese restaurant, video store
3. CVS Pharmacy
4. Kentucky Fried Chicken
5. United Methodist Church
6. Mobil gasoline station
7. Family Auto
8. Exxon gasoline station
9. Maryland Bank & Trust/Baldus Building
10. Baldus Real Estate administrative offices
11. True Value Hardware
12. Burger King
13. Gardiner Farm Equipment
14. Vacant house
15. Posey's Market
16. Rescue Squad
17. Wildes Printing
18. Mitchell's offices
19. Lawyer's office
20. Residence
21. Motrol electronics
22. Moghni Mosque
23. Hair salon
24. Creative Image hair salon
25. CPA firm/lawyers
26. Pien's hair salon
27. Flower shop
28. Lawyers' offices
29. Kara's nail salon
30. Mitchell's building supplies complex; Creative Kitchen Design
31. Lawyers' offices
32. Centennial Square
33. Martin's gas station, Jimmy's Car Wash
34. La Grange Building
35. Stained Glass shop
36. Doctors' offices
37. Lawyers' offices
38. County First Bank
39. Doctors' offices
40. Norris Building
41. Norris Building II
42. Bowling Building
43. Counseling center
44. CPA firm
45. Lawyers' offices
46. Commercial outbuildings
47-53. Residential
54. Time and Again clock shop
55-58. Residential
59. Texaco gasoline station and Dash-In store
60-68. Residential

— Molli Yood

The tornado left a nearly lateral east-west path of damage through the middle of town.

SOUTHERN MARYLAND EXTRA/SUNDAY, JUNE 16, 2002

6-15: *The LPTD legend.*

Fortunately, LPTD 1, the Archbishop Neale School (ANS), was not in session on Sunday, April 28, 2002, when the tornado struck. This was unlike the February 9, 1926, La Plata tornado, which struck an elementary school while it was in session.

The following aerial and ground views show the ANS damage incurred by the tornado. These photographs were submitted to the Charles County Government by Warren Robinette.

6-16: ANS *aerial damage view 1.*

6-17: ANS *aerial damage view 2.*

Tornado damaged the school in 2002

6-18: ANS *roof damage.*

6-19: ANS *exterior damage.*

6-20: ANS *damage viewed by school children 1.*

6-21: ANS *damage viewed by school children 2.*

6-22: ANS *interior damage*.

The following recollection by two sisters teaching at ANS was related to Victoria Weis in July 2008 and published in A WHIRLWIND OF STORIES, La Plata Tornado, 2002. Sisters Helene and Jane Mary are members of the Congregation of the Sisters, Servants of the Immaculate Heart of Mary headquartered in Scranton, Pennsylvania. The Sisters faithfully served the ANS in the Town of La Plata from 1927 to 2007.

Sisters Felt God's Protection

Sister Helene and I were at Marywood in Scranton, Pennsylvania for four days of community meetings. We had driven through dense fog in the Poconos. As we were driving down Route 301, we heard on the radio that there were thunderstorms and lightening in the Washington area. We arrived at the convent around 5:30 p.m, took our things into the house, and got settled. Sister Helene wanted to go over to ANS to check the mail because we had been gone for several days. She went to school and I started to get settled. I turned on the television and by that time Sister Helene was back from school. We were watching Channel 9 and "Topper" Shut was saying that the storm was heading north towards Washington, D.C. Sister Helene and I didn't think too much of it, we turned the television off.

I went to the third floor of the convent and Sister Helene was on the second floor. We were both unpacking our things. I called another Sister, who is a friend of mine that lives in Indiana, and was telling her about our meetings at Marywood. I told her that I might have to hang up because there was a storm in the area. Just as I said that, the lights started to flicker so I ended my call. Sister Helene had been looking out her bedroom window and she could see that the sky was getting black. All of a sudden there was this terrible noise that sounded like a freight train coming through the house. Sister Helene called up to me to come downstairs. I went down the stairs and met her at the bottom, though I don't remember ever touching the steps. We started to head toward the first floor of the convent trying to make our way to the basement, but the whole house started to shake and the noise became deafening. Our cat, Tangles, ran upstairs into the laundry room. Things started flying around and coming into the house so we couldn't go any further because we were afraid we would be hit by debris and broken glass. We stayed against the wall on the second floor between the wall and the banister to the stairs and just hugged each other. We had no idea what was going on; we weren't thinking tornado. At one point I didn't know if we were going to survive this or not. It was over in 40 seconds, definitely less than a minute. The last thing we remember is a picture flew off the wall at the other end of the hallway, landed at our feet, and smashed. It was a picture of "Jesus Knocking At The Door". Then everything stopped and there was a deafening silence and calm. I noticed it was 7:04 pm on the kitchen clock.

Helene looked out the kitchen window and said to me, "Brent Hall is gone." I thought to myself, "What does that mean?" We decided to go downstairs and open the front door. Meanwhile, I was on the phone trying to contact our superiors in Scranton, PA. We were afraid to open the front door because we didn't know what we would find. After we opened the door and went out, we saw that all of the cedar trees around the convent were broken in half like toothpicks, the statue of the Blessed Mother was lying flat on the ground, half of the porch was off, the windows on Sister Helene's car were blown out, and there were trees and debris everywhere. Debris had fallen in on the property, so we had to step over trees and we were conscious of the electrical wires that were lying on the ground. We slowly made our way around the front of the kindergarten wing of the school. The primary wing of the school had caved in and all the windows were broken. I went ahead of Helene and since we had just come back from a celebration at Marywood, I had my camera with me. I started taking pictures of the school. As we got to the front of the school, the damage got worse. We could see that Brent Hall was gone, there were stairs going up to nowhere and the bathrooms seemed to be hanging in midair. There were two automobiles on the property that were black and their windows were blown out. We didn't know where the cars had come from. The front of the school had collapsed and all the windows were smashed. We soon found out that the damage got worse when we went into the building. The school chapel was destroyed.

6-23: The ANS Sisters Story.

Author's note: The Sisters said in their narrative that they were watching Channel 9 (which is WUSA in Washington, D.C.) and that "Topper Shut" (his last name is actually spelled (Shutt) was saying that the storm was heading north towards Washington, D.C. Shutt claims that he never said that. Personally, I side with the good Sisters on that contentious point. By the way folks, Shutt claims (as reported in the May 1, 2002 issue of the *Maryland Independent*) that the "station preempted CBS's "60 Minutes" program in order to stay on the air with live coverage." To the best of my knowledge, that highly acclaimed program always aired on Sunday evening beginning at 7 p.m. At that time, the La Plata tornado was probably approaching the Archbishop Neale School after plummeting Quailwood. In my personal opinion, it seems a little too late for beginning "live coverage" of an already developed weather disaster.

A group of brave, supportive, and stoic ANS students posed in front of their heavily damaged school only two days after it was struck by the tornado.

6-24: *The stoic ANS students.*

After striking the Archbishop Neale School, the tornado now apparently sporting two vortexes, would simultaneously hit the La Plata Shopping Center and the United Methodist Church.

This hellish photograph taken by Kevin Clark with *The Washington Post* on the evening of Sunday, April 28, 2002, shows the destruction at these locations with the United Methodist Church seen to the left and a portion of the La Plata Shopping Center seen to the right.

6-25: *Night view of destruction.*

The following aerial photographs capture this destruction at these same two locations. The photographs were submitted to the Charles County Government by Warren Robinette on the morning of April 29, 2002.

In these photographs, notice the two vortex outline traces (VORTEX 1 and VORTEX 2) at these locations and the clogged traffic in both the north and south bound lanes of Route 301 (Crain Highway).

6-26: *The Two vortexes.*

The outline trace of VORTEX 2 can be seen better in the following aerial photograph.

6-27: VORTEX 2.

The nightmarish view on Tuesday morning (April 30, 2002), at the intersection of Routes 301 and 6, is reminiscent of a scene from the *Twilight Zone* episode, **"Time Enough at Last."**

6-28: Stark Tuesday morning.

The La Plata Shopping Center (LPTD 2) included the Bank of Southern Maryland, a flower shop (Davis' Florists), a dry cleaners (Annie's Discount Cleaners), a carryout Chinese restaurant (East Coast Chinese), and a video store (Video Unlimited), which were all ravaged by F3 force winds.

6-29: *The La Plata Shopping Center.*

The next series of photographs were taken by Dawn Glencer of the damaged businesses at the La Plata Shopping Center. Note the police guarding the damaged Bank of Southern Maryland. Receipts, checks, and tax documents from the bank were recovered nearly seventy miles away in Seaford, Delaware.

6-30: *Guarding an empty bank?*

The CVS Pharmacy (LPDT 3) and its sign, located at the intersection of Routes 301 and 6, were severely damaged and ravaged by the F3 tornado. The pharmacy lost its roof while its sign was mangled into twisted metal.

6-31: **X** *marks the spot.*

6-32: *The CVS sign.*

The following is only an excerpt from a riveting story told to Victoria A. Weiss by William Wikert. The entire story appeared in the 2009 publication, A WHIRLWOOD OF STORIES, La Plata Tornado, 2002, in August 2008.

Father and Daughter in Tornado Together

On the day of the tornado I went to CVS to buy a belated birthday card for my father. On the north side of Route 6, coming toward La Plata, the sky was dark blue. It looked like a storm was coming but on the south side, it was bright and sunny. I had no idea that there was a tornado warning. I parked about eight car-lengths away from CVS, facing Safeway. I went into CVS, bought the card, came out and put my two-year old daughter in her car seat in the back on the passenger's side. When I turned around and was facing CVS, I could see the tornado behind CVS. As soon as I saw that, I slammed the door shut, got in the car, and my first thought was to get out of the eye of the tornado. I was directly in the eye.

I quickly made a U-turn and when I did that it put me directly in front of the CVS doors right against the curb. By that time, things were hitting my windshield so hard that it seemed like someone was taking a sledgehammer to my car. I couldn't see what was hitting it because of all the dust; it was like we were in a fog. I slammed my foot on the brake, turned around and threw my daughter's car seat on its side, and I leaned in between the two front seats. When I threw my daughter down, I took my foot off the brake and since I never put it in park, the car started to move. I slammed the car into park and at that time the roof of CVS just collapsed. All of a sudden, the roof of CVS landed on my car and you could hear the top of my car going down; it sounded like a creaky door hinge. I was in between the seats and my daughter was on the floorboards on the back seat. I was watching the roof of my car coming down and it came down to the shoulder rest and then it stopped. I thanked God because that was about where I was and if it had gone further I would have been stuck. If our car had been two or three feet away from the curb, the peak of the CVS roof would have come down on top of the car, which would have collapsed the roof even more.

6-33: The Wikert story.

The Kentucky Fried Chicken (KFC) restaurant (LPTD 4), located in the parking lot of the La Plata Shopping Center, was heavily damaged. It lost two of its retaining walls. The photograph was taken by Dawn Glencer.

6-34: KFC.

Tables and chairs at the KFC restaurant were left open to the elements after the storm struck. Supposedly, a dish of fried chicken remained intact on one of the tables. In the foreground, the faintly lit Mobil gas station (center) and the United Methodist Church (right) can be seen. This photograph was taken by James A. Parcell for *The Washington Post*.

6-35: *The KFC open air restaurant.*

In an article which appeared in the Monday, April 29, 2002, edition of *The Washington Post*, Francis Barnes Jr., of Waldorf reports that he was working at KFC that night when a customer pulled up to the drive-through window and warned that a funnel cloud was coming. At almost the same moment, the storm struck the building, which had about twenty people inside at the time. "Everybody started screaming, 'Get down, get down,'" Barnes said. "Glass was everywhere." People fled the building. A woman shouted to Barnes to grab her baby. He picked up the child, and the woman snatched up her other young children. Together, all five ran out the back of the restaurant.

The United Methodist Church (LPTD 5) lost its steeple, sanctuary, and education hall. In addition, a number of vehicles parked in its lot were heavily damaged. The following photographs were taken by Dawn Glencer. Fortunately, Sunday services were held at 8:30 a.m. and 11:00 a.m. on April

28, 2002, so the church and parking lot were relatively empty at the time the tornado struck.

6-36: *The church without a steeple.*

6-37: *The church parking lot.*

6-38: *Aerial view of the church's damage.*

6-39: *Vehicle turned into a convertible.*

6-40: *Rosary beads still hanging inside car.*

In addition to this damage, the tornado blew out a stained-glass window in the church sanctuary itself, as well as destroying a number of others. This photograph, taken by Lawrence Jackson, Jr., a staff photographer with the *Maryland Independent* newspaper, shows parishioners struggling to rescue the blown-out window.

6-41: *Rescued stained glass window.*

Finally, the roof of the Blessed Lamb Preschool, located on the grounds of the Methodist Church, was blown-off. Fortunately, it being a Sunday evening, the school was not in session. Notice the missing steeple blown off the church. It was found lying in the front yard of the church grounds.

6-42: *Blessed Lamb Preschool.*

The Mobil gas station (LPTD 6), located at the southwest corner of Routes 6 and 301, suffered severe damage as the F3 tornado crossed this intersection at approximately 7:02 p.m.

The hardest hit segments at the gas station were the pumps and the service building.

6-43: *Damage at the Mobil gas station.*

This is a photograph of the wiring spaghetti piled in front of the Mobil station after being torn from the pumps and other electrical conduits. The damaged Deluxe Inn Motel can be seen in the background.

6-44: Spaghetti wiring.

Next door to the Mobil gas station was the Deluxe Inn Motel. It incurred damage to its roof and entrance.

6-45: Roof damage at the Deluxe Inn Motel.

6-46: *Entrance damage at the Deluxe Inn Motel.*

The Exxon gas station (LPTD 8), and its Tiger Mart convenience store, located at the northeast corner of Routes 301 and 6 (Charles Street), was battered by F3/F4 force wings as the tornado crossed Route 301. This photograph was taken by Marty Martin.

6-47: *The Exxon and Tiger Mart.*

6-48: *The Exxon and Tiger Mart, another view.*

Directly across the street from the Exxon gas station was the Maryland Bank and Trust Company building (LPTD 9), which suffered major damage to its façade.

6-49: *The Maryland Bank and Trust.*

Right next to the Maryland Bank and Trust, at 101 East Charles Street, was the Baldus Realty building (LPTD 10), which was severely damaged.

6-50: *Baldus Realty.*

Working the night of the tornado at Baldus Realty was Bonnie Baldus Grier, who related her personal story in the Town of La Plata's **Memory Lane Exhibit**:

Bonnie Baldus Grier was working in the office on that Sunday evening trying to finish up a real estate contract for a client. "The lights flashed and I hit the save button on the computer," she recalled. "I looked out the back door of the office but I looked the wrong way. If I had gone out and looked from the parking lot out front I would have seen the darn thing coming. I looked out the window and I saw horizontal debris flying by," she said. "I got down on my stomach and covered my head and it just hit. After awhile I got up and opened the door to my office and the second wave hit so I hit the deck again."

Bonnie was extremely lucky that she was not seriously injured when the tornado hit the building. "When it was done I looked down the hall and I saw an 8-foot hole in the roof. I could see daylight," she said. "It shattered all of the windows in the front and stuff was blown everywhere."

6-51: *Bonnie's Story.*

More of Bonnie's amazing story was reported in the Friday, April 25, 2003, **SPECIAL EDITION** of the *Maryland Independent* in an article written by Sara K. Taylor, a staff writer with the newspaper.

SPECIAL EDITION: A town on the rebound

Tornado touched friends and neighbors

Realtor poised to rebuild

BY SARA K. TAYLOR
STAFF WRITER

It isn't unusual for Bonnie Baldus Grier to work Sundays in her La Plata real estate office. And the evening of April 28, 2002, she was working on a contract for clients when a storm was coming.

"The lights flashed and went out," she said. "But they came right back on."

Grier looked out a back door and saw blue skies dotted with clouds; everything seemed serene.

The tornado was coming up behind her.

"If I looked the other way, I probably would have had a heart attack," she said.

On the way back to her office the lights flickered again. She saw a car pull up in the Baldus parking lot and debris swirling in the air. "Somewhere in the recesses of my mind I thought, 'Get away from the windows,'" Grier said. She started shutting every office door before lying face down in a hallway, covering her head with her arms.

"I can't remember any sound," she said. "I think I have blocked all of it out, but I remember the noise stopping, and I opened the door to my office when I heard a loud noise and

ing or if I was praying."

Holes were ripped throughout the ceiling, with office furniture and supplies everywhere. Grier wasn't so much as scratched, having worn long pants and a long-sleeve shirt.

She made her way to the office's entrance, and once outside saw people walking around, out of their cars — dazed.

"I thought nobody is going to believe this, I better take some pictures," Grier said. She reached into her car — the windows were blown out, so it was easy — and got her camera.

She wandered around La Plata, taking pictures and listening to police scanners, when she thought of her brother, Rick, and his wife, Margy, who lived behind the county government building.

The police weren't letting anyone across U.S. 301, so Grier walked farther down and when no one was looking crossed the street.

"I spent a while just kind of wandering through the town of La Plata," she said.

She ended up spending the night with Rick's in-laws before going home to her Rose Hill Road house that also suffered extensive damage — including about 50 acres of trees uprooted.

For a while after the tornado, Grier said she was spooked whenever the weather was stormy, but she's getting better about it.

"Life goes on," Grier said. "You pick up the pieces and move on."

STAFF PHOTO BY GARY SMITH

Bonnie Baldus Grier stands outside the temporary Baldus Real Estate offices just up Charles Street from where she was working April 28 last year when the tornado hit La Plata.

knew another one was coming."

She shut the door and resumed her prostrate position.

"It was probably only a matter of seconds, but it felt longer," Grier said. "I don't know if I was crying, scream-

6-52: *More of Bonnie's story.*

To the right of the Maryland Bank and Trust bank on Route 301 was the True Value Hardware store (LPTD 11), which was also heavily damaged.

6-53: *The True Value store.*

Continuing south on Route 301, and next to the True Value store, was the heavily damaged Burger King (LPTD 12).

6-54: Burger King.

Traveling up Charles Street, one found the remains of the renowned Posey's Market (LPTD 15). It was in business for eleven years as a mom and pop establishment, and the favorite grocery store of the author. The staff was always friendly and they had the best fresh-cut meat in town.

The curbside sign for the market stood relatively untouched after the tornado struck. Its marquee still said, "GENUINE SO MD STUFFED HAM, $7.98 LB."

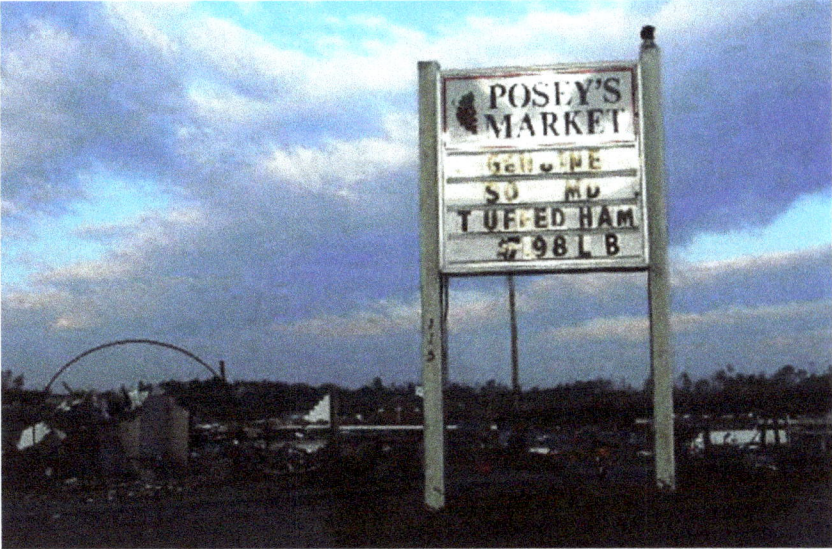

6-55: *Posey's Market sign.*

However, the Posey's Market building behind the sign was a pile of sticks and rubble.

6-56: *What was left of Posey's Market.*

The store would eventually be leveled. It never reopened due to high cost of rebuilding and the strong competitive market in place at that time from large supermarkets within La Plata. It was truly a sad day for the author.

The Charles County Rescue Squad (LPTD 16), located at 2 Calvert Street, was heavily damaged by the passage of the tornado, thus limiting its ability to assist during the immediate emergency response phase and then a little later during the series of search and rescue operations. The facility's ambulances were stored there. Even more important, access to the building was blocked by debris. It was some time before ambulances could get out of the building to treat and transport the injured. By a stroke of good fortune, one of the Rescue Squad BLS units was on Route 301 several miles north of La Plata when the tornado went through. This ambulance was returning from a call in Waldorf, and responded immediately to the intersection of Route 301 and 6 where many of the injured were concentrated. A number of mutual aid ambulances from other area rescue stations also responded during both the immediate emergency response, and the search and rescue operation phases following the disaster.

6-57: *The Charles County Rescue Squad.*

Further up the road on Charles Street, the La Plata Volunteer Fire Department building suffered broken windows. There was also debris everywhere.

6-58: *The La Plata Volunteer Fire Department building.*

Irene Spalding's home on Howard Street was severely damaged by trees collapsing on top of the brick residence. Her ailing husband was pinned within.

6-59: *Irene Spalding's house.*

Irene Spalding's touching story was told to Victoria Weiss, in September 2008, for her publication, A WHIRLWIND OF STORIES, La Plata Tornado, 2002.

"Miracle Man" and His Wife Survive Tornado

My husband was in a hospital bed in our bedroom. He hadn't eaten or spoken for four days. Father Matt, Pastor of Sacred Heart Church, had come to visit him on Thursday and gave him communion. Father Matt told me that he was asking people to pray for a peaceful death for my husband. Sunday, April 28, I was in our bedroom with my husband and I was holding his hand. The television was on but my husband still wasn't talking. I heard on the television that there was a tornado headed for Waldorf. If I had looked behind me out our bedroom window, I would have seen the tornado.

I told my husband that I would be right back. I turned the television off and unplugged it. The sky had gotten very dark. I walked into the kitchen and at that time, the tornado blew the back door open, the porch was blown away, and I was picked up and thrown under the dining room table. The shelf on the dining room wall must have fallen down before I was thrown because it knocked me unconscious and broke my heel.

I don't know how long I was out but when I came to, I got up to check on my husband and he said, "Where have you been? I have been calling you." I went into the bedroom and my husband had three bricks and insulation on his head. I know their were three because I was the one who pulled the bricks off of him. My daughter saved the bricks and to this day still has them. One of the trees in the yard had gone straight through the bedroom wall. By that time, the rescue squad was coming over. You couldn't get through the front door; you had to crawl. The rescue squad people picked up my husband and put him in another room because the bed he was in was so bad. We couldn't get out of the house until the next day when someone came and sawed the trees off the front porch.

The next day the ambulance came but they couldn't get down Howard Street, which is where I live. They put my husband and me on stretchers and took us over to the rescue squad and we got into the ambulance. My husband's head was severely cut but it was too late to stitch him up so they just let it heal on its own. I was in the hospital for a week because of my broken heel.

My husband said later that he had heard the sound of the train but I didn't hear anything. We had lots of stuff in our yard; we even had someone's sofa. No one knows where all that stuff came from. The tornado broke every window in the basement. Even though all the windows in my house aside from one were blown out, the china except for a few tea cups in my dining room was never touched. We had a statue of the Blessed Mother in our backyard that we never found.

My husband lived a year and four months after the tornado. He was able to walk with a walker and even carry on a small conversation with someone. Every time Father Matt would walk in the door he would say, "Where's my miracle man?"

I will never forget the tornado.

Irene Spalding
As told to Victoria Weiss
September 2008

6-60: Irene's story.

An article which appeared in the Tuesday, April 30, 2002, issue of The Washington Post METRO section tells the story of parishioners at the Christ Church when the tornado hit during a planning meeting.

MARC FISHER

Across La Plata, Seeing Blessings Amid Wreckage

The sky turned yellow, then black, a wasp's nest of wicked weather. The wind sounded like a Sensurround epic, only real. Everyone's cell phones started brrringing at once. Then darkness and an awkward search for the basement.

A dozen members of Christ Church in La Plata had gathered for a Sunday evening meeting to plan a trip to Ground Zero in New York City to help those who've been ministering to rescue workers at the World Trade Center site. Then Ground Zero came to La Plata.

"We were working out the cost of the hotels," said Jerry Anderson, one of the parishioners, when suddenly, right after 7 p.m., the basement beckoned. "The glass began to break, and we started moving."

6-61: Christ Church article.

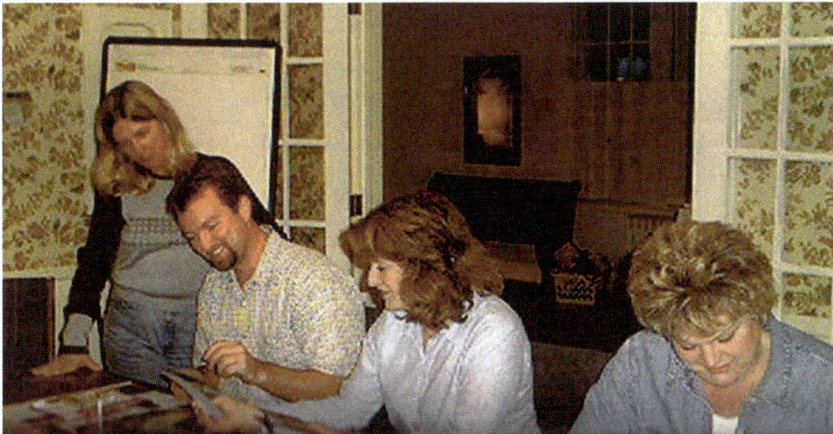

6-62: Planning meeting at Christ Church.

The tornado caused extensive damage to the roof of the Parish House and downed multiple trees all around the church property.

6-63: *Damage to the Christ Church Parish House.*

6-64: *Close-up view of damage to the roof of Parish House.*

Before we continue with our journey through the destruction of downtown La Plata, let us look at an aerial view of this area looking northwest on April 29, 2002. This region was alternately battered with F3 and F4 force winds. The photograph was taken by James M. Thresher for *The Washington Post.*

6-65: *Aerial view of downtown La Plata looking northwest on April 29, 2002.*

Tim Marshall from Haag Engineering saw lots of evidence of F4 damage on St. Mary's Avenue and La Grange Avenue.

6-66: F4 damage in downtown La Plata.

The following aerial and ground photographs show the buckled and collapsed seventy-five-thousand gallon La Plata water tower off St. Mary's Avenue.

6-67: Aerial view, La Plata water tower.

6-68: *Water tower, down and out.*

The one-hundred-year-old tower was located on the north end of the tornado damage path. According to Timothy P. Marshall with the Haag Engineering Company, "Four steel legs buckled and the tower fell to the southwest, sending a torrent of water that flooded three houses. Each leg was attached to a concrete footing with a single bolt. Bolts on the north legs failed in tension, leading to the collapse of the tower." Because of its design, the tower fell in an area where F1 damage occurred to wood-framed buildings. The fallen water tower deprived most of the downtown La Plata area of its water supply.

Mitchell's Supply (LPTD 30), located on St. Mary's Avenue, was struck by F4 winds. There was severe damage to the store itself, while the attached lumber yard (situated to the right of the store) created a debris field of flying lumber and other building material. Numerous buildings and homes downwind of its location were destroyed, especially on La Grange Avenue and Maple Avenue.

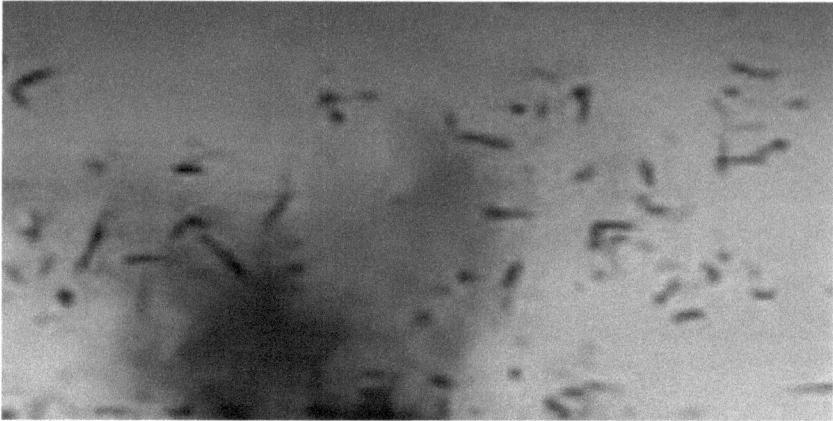

6-69: *Flying lumber and debris.*

In fact, this damage area was initially classified as the F5 level until a National Weather Service Storm Survey Team determined that in this particular area, much of the damage was caused not by the wind velocity, but by flying debris from the lumber yard. So, the damage area was downgraded to an F4 instead. In addition, in this and in other residential areas, split-level homes that were leveled by the tornado contained fatal structural flaws, which caused them to fail in less than F5 level winds.

The following photographs show two different views of Mitchell's Supply, including both the mostly hardware store and the adjoining lumber yard. The first view is looking south towards St. Mary's Avenue and the second view is on St. Mary's Avenue looking west towards Charles Street.

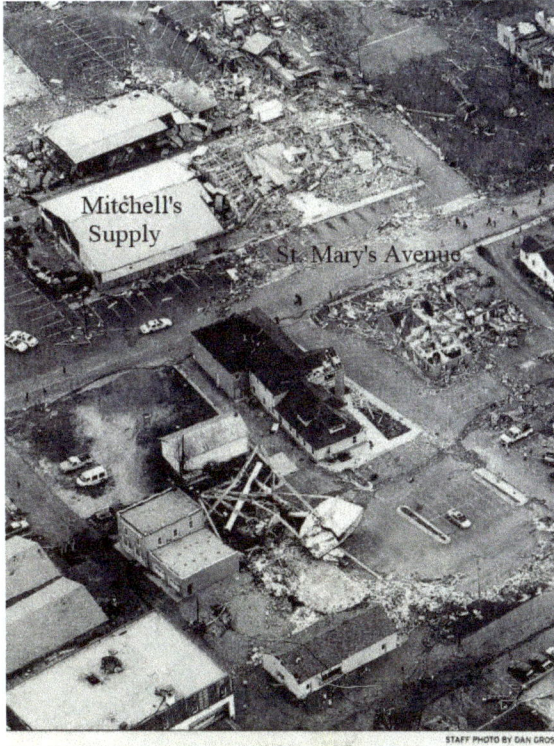

6-70: *Mitchell's Supply looking south.*

6-71: *Mitchell's Supply looking north.*

The tornado was moving from left to the lower right in the following picture. La Grange Avenue goes from the lower left corner up to Charles Street near the top of the picture. The heavy F4 damage streak enters the left of the picture and moves right towards the railroad tracks.

6-72: *Track of debris field from Mitchell's Supply.*

Here is another view of the downwind debris damage. It was caused by the flying lumber and building supplies from Mitchell's Supply, directed towards the residences located on La Grange Avenue and Maple Avenue. This picture was taken from above Route 301 looking east. Charles Street/ Route 6 moves up the left center of the picture. The tornado path moved up the left-center and to the right center of the picture.

6-73: *The tornado path.*

The home of Ed Middleton, located at 118 St. Mary's Avenue, incurred severe damage due to fallen trees. His home is located across from the Sacred Heart Church and down the street from the current site of the La Plata Star Sculpture located on Queen Anne Street.

6-74: *Home of Ed Middleton.*

LPTD 33, Martin's gas station, is located at 309 Charles Street in La Plata. Martin's has been a family owned and operated business serving the Town of La Plata and the surrounding area since 1922. This year marks the one-hundredth anniversary of this establishment. Marty and Caroline Martin are the proud owners of a third generation business. Marty's father and grandfather worked hard to provide automotive repair service and fuel to the people of southern Maryland.

Marty Martin shared his reaction to the destruction of his business with Jay Friess, a staff reporter with the *Maryland Independent* newspaper. The story was printed in the Wednesday, May 1, 2002, issue of the paper:

Marty Martin gazed on the crumbling remains of Martin's, the gas station his family has operated at 309 Charles St. in La Plata since 1922.

"It's unreal," he said in disbelief. "Unreal."

One of his relatives handed him two plastic funnels Monday morning that were lying in the parking lot.

"They're probably scattered all over town," he joked bitterly.

Martin's office survived with a blown out window. However, the attached garage was on the verge of collapse Monday, being supported only by the steel frame of the station's car lift.

Martin hoped to get his tow truck and his expensive diagnostic machines out of the garage before the structure was condemned and bulldozed.

JAY FRIESS

6-75: *Marty's story.*

The following photographs, given to me by Marty Martin, show the severe damage caused by the tornado to the outside and inside of his Charles Street establishment.

The sheer destruction of the tornado is clearly seen in this side view taken by Marty.

6-76: The station is torn asunder.

The service bays are hardly recognizable due to the damage from the tornado. The back wall has disappeared, but the automotive diagnostic and testing gear along the back wall was able to weather the storm. The two service bay lifts luckily caught the roof trusses, which enabled that portion of the roof to hold in place and not collapse, at least for a while, until salvage operations could remove much of the expensive diagnostic and testing equipment in the service bay.

6-77: The service bays.

This photograph, looking towards Charles Street, clearly shows that the damage was severe and widespread throughout the station. Notice that the roof of the white truck has caught the back of building's roof, preventing that portion of the roof from collapsing onto the service bay below.

6-78: *A view of the destruction looking towards Charles Street.*

Martin's marquee advertises the WALK AMERICA event held earlier on the very day of the tornado.

6-79: *The WALK AMERICA marquee.*

One of the three service bays at Martin's, nearest the front entrance, was the overnight home of Marty's tow truck. The glass overhead door to the bay was collapsed inward by the passing tornado, and its debris covered the truck. However, Marty was able to remove the debris and drive the tow truck out. He was able to use the tow truck for an additional three years. In 2005, he traded it in for a new one.

6-80: *Save the tow truck for another day.*

Jimmy's car wash was located right behind Martin's. The building literally collapsed during its encounter with the tornado. The filmy sheet metal-constructed building couldn't withstand the fierce winds of the tornado. The structure was never rebuilt after the storm and the enterprise folded.

6-81: *Jimmy's Car Wash.*

The historic home of Sidney Mudd was located on the northeast corner of St. Mary's and Centennial Street with an address of 106 St. Mary's Avenue.

MUDD, Sidney Emanuel, (son of Sidney Emanuel Mudd [1858–1911]), a Representative from Maryland; born at "Gallant Green," Charles County, Md., June 20, 1885; attended the public schools of Charles County and the District of Columbia; moved with his parents to La Plata, Md., in 1896; was graduated from the academic department of Georgetown University, Washington, D.C., in 1906 and from the law department in 1909; unsuccessful candidate for election to the Maryland house of delegates in 1909; was admitted to the bar in 1910; professor of criminal law at Georgetown University Law School in 1910; appointed assistant district attorney of the District of Columbia in February 1911 and resigned in March 1912; unsuccessful candidate for nomination in 1912 for election to the Sixty-third Congress; reappointed assistant district attorney in July 1912 and resigned in March 1914, to become a candidate for Congress; elected as a Republican to the Sixty-fourth and to the four succeeding Congresses and served from March 4, 1915, until his death in Baltimore, Md., October 11, 1924; interment in St. Ignatius' Catholic Church Cemetery, Chapel Point, near La Plata, Charles County, Md.

6-82: *Biographic Sketch of Sydney Emanuel Mudd.*

The Mudd home was severely damaged by the tornado, so much that it was beyond repair. However, it was rebuilt using the same basic design as the original home.

6-83: *The damaged Mudd home.*

The Mudd home was featured in a video, which was basically a walking tour of the damaged downtown La Plata area with the then Mayor of La Plata, William Eckman. He was accompanied by Bruce Johnson, an anchorman and reporter with WUSA 9 (CBS) television in Washington, D.C.

See:

https://search.aol.com/aol/video;_ylt=AwrE19fS.
P9gRLwAMjNpCWVH;_ylu=Y29sbwNiZjEEcG9zAzEEdnRpZAMEc2V-
jA3Nj?q=la+plata+tornado&v_t=comsearch#id=18&vid=ee49542aeb-
4fe99f477583c0dde72a7d&action=view

As we continue our own damage tour through downtown La Plata, we move east up Centennial Street and find the heavily damaged County First Bank (LPTD 38) at 202 Centennial Street.

6-84: *The County First Bank.*

The then Centennial Street Development building, located at 305 Centennial Street, was also badly damaged by the passage of the tornado.

6-85: *The Centennial Street Development Building.*

As mentioned earlier, the properties located on La Grange and South Maple Avenues suffered both from the direct effects of the F3/F4 tornado winds, and from the effects of flying debris, especially from the lumber yard located at Mitchell's Supply located on St. Mary's Avenue. Properties on either side if this center path were damaged by pockets of F1 force winds. Tim Marshall with Haag Engineering provided this diagram of this assessment.

6-86: *Meteorological assessment.*

At the corner of Charles Street and La Grange Avenue stood the Bowling building (LPTD 42), a quaint merchandise and variety store. Like many such establishments, it suffered major damage to its roof. Note the damaged La Plata Post Office seen to the left, further down the street on La Grange Avenue.

6-87: *The Bowling building.*

The original La Plata Post Office building, located at 101 La Grange Avenue, suffered major roof damage.

6-88: *The La Plata Post Office.*

The La Grange building (LPTD 34) was located at 109 La Grange Avenue. The tenants occupying the second floor were displaced when that portion of the building collapsed.

6-89: *The La Grange building.*

The following photographs, taken by Barbara Watson, show the aftermath of the tornado for those residential properties located at 112-114 La Grange Avenue in downtown La Plata.

6-90: *112 La Grange Avenue.*

6-91: 113 La Grange Avenue.

6-92: 114 La Grange Avenue.

Probably one of the most endearing and touching photographs taken in the aftermath of the La Plata tornado was the one taken by Andrea Bruce for *The Washington Post*.

6-93: *John Sherbert rescuing items from his home.*

The photograph shows John Sherbert, proudly wearing his Washington Redskins cap, and Ronnie Taylor the morning after the tornado, collecting important papers and documents in the ruins of his collapsed house on Edelan Station Place.

Additional photographs of John's home can be seen in the following montage.

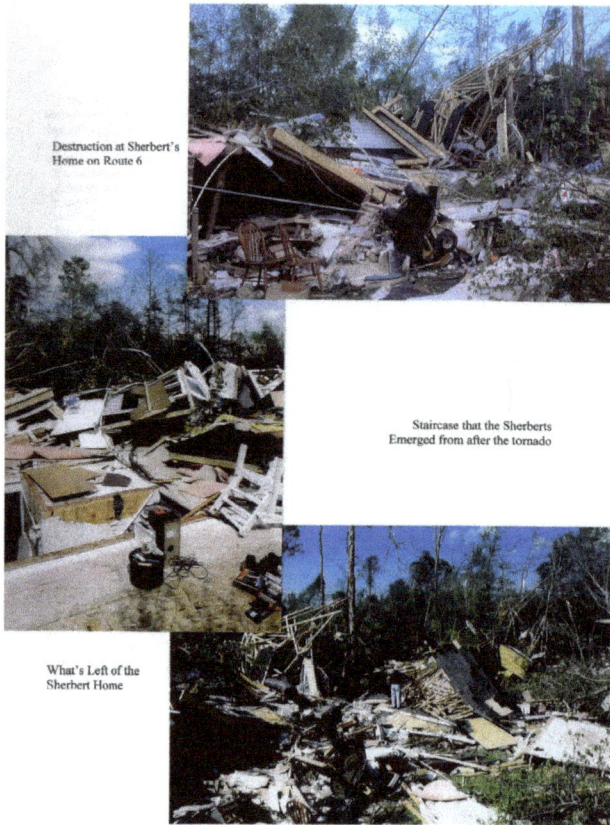

Destruction at Sherbert's Home on Route 6

Staircase that the Sherberts Emerged from after the tornado

What's Left of the Sherbert Home

6-94: *Montage of the damage to the Sherbert home.*

John told his stirring story to Victoria Weiss in September 2008 for the publication, A WHIRLWIND OF STORIES, La Plata Tornado, 2002.

Emergency Training Pays Off

We were home the afternoon when the tornado hit. We had finished dinner and were watching TV. We began to have a series of brown outs with the electricity and then the weather reported a tornado had touched down in Port Tobacco, heading due east. With that, the TV went out and then the power went within a couple seconds.

Our youngest, Donny ran to the front window, I was right behind him. Donald saw the tornado coming in the front yard; he was the only one that saw it. At the time our front yard had well over one hundred oak trees, now there are approximately fifteen. As we reached our basement Donny and I saw a large oak tree hit the ground. We knew it was going to be very serious as we saw the same tree lift off the ground and disappear.

One of the things that we realized was that our kids knew where to go more so than we did. We realized that all the school training you get about emergencies was actually paying off. We went into the basement, then, into a front room that is below ground level. We shut the door. As we were going into the room the tornado was on top of us. People describe tornadoes as like being on a freight train. I describe it as like sitting on the engine of a 747 on takeoff. There was a high pitch to it. We heard the tornado take the house down. The thing I vividly remember from the storm is the sound—the snapping of the two by fours of the house. Just snapping and snapping and snapping. It was over in twenty to twenty-five seconds. It was so quick. We said a prayer when we got into the room; we said a prayer while the tornado was going over. After the tornado had passed I went into the basement living room. I decided to have everyone stay in the room while I made sure it was safe to come out. After looking around for a few seconds I returned to the room where my family was waiting. I told them it was very bad but everything would be okay as we were all unharmed. We said another prayer.

We were in a two story house with a finished basement. Both of the top levels were gone; most of the house was in the backyard. Thirty minutes after the tornado all you could hear were chain saws. People were straddling live power lines, cutting trees so that rescue workers could make their way into our community. The community really came together after the tornado.

The next morning we went into a post tornado mode. We had to clean up the debris, find a place to live and purchase all of the necessities that are required. We were very fortunate because we were able to save all of our photo albums. We lost a lot of individual pictures. Our last photo album, our son found in the backyard about two weeks after the tornado hit. We never found our bathtub, our washer and dryer. We have people that will come over and say when you go to Sherbert's house look up because the washer might be coming down. The tornado just pushed all of our stuff into the backyard. There was a lot of debris. We had a No Parking sign in our yard from the parking lot where the Baldus building is now.

One of the long lasting effects that we still deal with is when there are storms in the area we pay close attention to the weather. We don't take any storm for granted anymore.

A week after the tornado hit we were out clearing debris. A school bus pulled into our small development. People started exiting the bus, they were like ants walking towards my lot.. About forty people hopped off the bus with chain saws, shovels, saws, and rakes and they just walked up to the yard and asked me "where can we start?" They worked for three or four hours and then went to the next place.

The day after the tornado, my nephew and I were outside cleaning up and a photographer from the Washington Post asked us if she could take some pictures of us. We said sure and the following day there was a picture of us on the front page of the Washington Post. In the picture I was wearing a Redskins hat. About a week later, the photographer called us and said that Dan Snyder wanted to do something for us from the Washington Redskins. He sent us a care package with shirts, jerseys, hats, jackets, and gloves. It was very nice.

The tornado hit on April 28, 2002 and we moved back into our new home on May 3, 2003. We built a totally different house but still have that room in the front available, just in case...

John Sherbert
As told to Victoria Weiss
September 2008

6-95: John Sherbert's story.

Sadly, John Alan Sherbert died on May 8, 2012, just ten years after his *Post* photograph was taken and nine years after finally moving back into his new home. John was an avid Washington Redskins fan, as well as being long-time supporter of local youth and high school sports. RIP John.

At the intersection of Charles Street and Maple Avenue, and bordering the railroad tracks, was the location of a favorite meeting place for the socially active young town people of the town (I am told), the Casey Jones Restaurant. The restaurant, located at 417 Charles Street, was moderately damaged by the passage of the tornado.

6-96: *The Casey Jones Restaurant.*

This view, taken from vantage point of the Casey Jones Restaurant, shows the heavy F3 residential damage on Oak Street and Wicomico Street across the railroad tracks. The photograph was provided courtesy of Mary Martin.

6-97: *Residential damage seen on Oak and Wicomico Streets.*

The home of Ann Davis is located behind the Casey Jones Restaurant on Maple Avenue. It suffered severe structural damage as the tornado passed.

6-98: *The Home of Ann Davis.*

Ronald "Gas" Perry Johnson lived at 100 Oak Avenue in La Plata when the tornado struck. He had lived in the two-story house that he inherited from his family since his birth on May 1, 1954. His residence was among the hardest hit, ripped apart like a dollhouse with many of its belongings scattered in the front and back yards. Fortunately, neither Johnson nor his son Jonathan "Lee" Johnson were at home at the time the tornado struck shortly after 7 p.m. the night of April 28, 2002. However, his tenant was in the house. His story was related in a Special Edition of the *Maryland Independent*, dated Wednesday, May 1, 2002, in an article written by Dallas Cogle, a staff writer with the paper.

"The guy that was in this room," Johnson said while pointing to the second-floor deck now lying in his back yard. "He had come home from work. He was watching TV and heard the tornado coming. He looked out the window, and then headed for the doorway of his bedroom. When he hit the door, the whole room fell behind him and sucked him back out and threw him down to the ground. The door shattered into little bits and pieces."

6-99: The tenant's experience.

In this touching photograph, Ron is embraced and comforted by a friend as he views the damage to his home along with his son Jonathan.

6-100: Ron being comforted.

This photograph of Ron Johnson standing in front of his heavily damaged home was taken by Dallas Cogle for the *Maryland Independent.*

6-101: Ron standing in front of his damaged home.

Ron sadly passed on February 15, 2015, at the age of sixty. During his life, he worked as a carpenter for CSI Worldwide LLC. He loved the outdoors and was an avid hunter and fisherman. He was a car enthusiast and loved to be in his workshop doing woodworks. RIP Ron.

Three seconds of the tornado devastated a Maryland couple's 1893 Victorian home located at 104 Oak Avenue. It was the beloved home of Tom and Jane O'Farrell, who now live in Hagerstown, Maryland. They were in Champaign, Illinois at the time of the tornado when their son, Steve, frantically called them. Can one imagine having to drive home some nine-hundred miles, thinking the whole time about what you would find when you arrived home?

The news came in a phone call: **"Dad, you better get back quick."** Our son Steve had called to tell us what he had just seen on TV. An F4 tornado with 240-mile-per-hour winds had ripped through the La Plata, Maryland, neighborhood where my wife, Jane, and I live. I sat stunned and helpless 900 miles away, on what was supposed to be a relaxing visit with family in Illinois.

"And the house?" I asked.

"Be prepared," came the reply.

THE SHOCK

We drove all night, expecting the worst. Of course, nothing could prepare us for the devastation we found. Our 1893 Folk Victorian stood directly in the storm's two-block path. The garage, which housed my woodworking shop, was gone, along with 47 trees. Our two chimneys were toppled, and the metal roof peeled away like a sardine can. The front and back of the balloon-frame house were bowed out, clapboards tains poking out. In the front upstairs bathroom, where a 2x4 had impaled the outer wall, debris had blasted the porcelain right off the tub. But in one of those freak-of-nature occurrences you sometimes get with a tornado, not a single piece of Jane's Dresden china collection was disturbed in the dining room, even though there were shards of window glass embedded in the walls and furniture. And of the upstairs bedrooms, only the front one was badly damaged.

6-102: *The O'Farrell's story.*

The following account was posted by reporter Frederick N. Rasmussen for the November 9, 2009 edition of *The Baltimore Sun.* The special edition presented an account of the deadly F4 La Plata tornado of November 9, 1926, as well as the F4 La Plata tornado of April 28, 2002, as seen through the eyes of an actual eyewitness to both events. In this special edition, Rasmussen related an interview he had with Irene Elizabeth Bowie Wood back in 2002, following the passage of the La Plata tornado of April 28, 2002. For Wood, Sunday's tornado was especially disturbing. It rekindled memories of La Plata's other devastating storm. The storm that struck on November 9, 1926, killed seventeen people, including thirteen children in the elementary school. Wood's sister, Mary Ellen Bowie, was among those killed. Irene B. Wood couldn't believe that it was happening again.

A lifelong La Plata resident, Wood, 86, was watching TV in her home on Oak Avenue early Sunday evening when the sky began to grow dark. She got up from her chair to make her way to the basement after seeing a storm warning broadcast.

"I looked at the clock. It was six minutes after seven," she said. "I was on my way to the basement when it came, and I only got as far as the dining room. I sort of froze there." She never got downstairs. Instead, she witnessed the ferocity of the winds.

"I kept hearing something hit the side of the house. As the widows cracked and broke, I just prayed. I lost electricity, phone, and my home was damaged," said Wood, who had been hospitalized in recent weeks for congestive heart failure. "But I thank God that I'm alive. I still get emotional when I think about it."

In Sunday's storm, Wood's brick home lost all its windows, several holes were torn in the roof and a porch column collapsed.

"It's eerie. There is glass everywhere but not a thing out of place in the house," said Betty Carney, her daughter. She attributes the house's survival to sound construction by her father, Harry F. Wood, who built it in 1937.

"Nothing moved or broke in the house, not one knick-knack or piece of furniture moved during the storm," she said. "It's the way it's always been."

Irene B. Wood was eighty-six-years-old when she did the 2002 Rasmussen interview. Irene was born on July 14, 1915, and died at the age of ninety-three on February 1, 2009. She would live long enough to experience, first hand, both the November 9, 1926, and the April 28, 2002, tornadoes.

Before we leave Oak Avenue, let's take a brief respite and look at a scene of someone mowing the lawn of Sam Phillips and Holly Dunbar, who once lived at 105 Oak Avenue.

Steve Gelzer of Indian Head, Charles County, mows the lawn of friends Sam Phillips and Holly Dunbar on Oak Avenue in La Plata, next to a house severely damaged by Sunday's tornado. (Sun photo by Karl Merton Ferron)

6-103: The grass still grows.

The Texaco gasoline station and Dash-In store (LPTD 59), on the southeast corner of Charles Street and Oak Avenue (601 Charles Street) was extensively damaged by the tornado, which tore off the roof of the store, thus exposing its merchandise to the elements. In order to salvage its contents, the proprietors decided to give away the merchandise before it was ruined by the weather. According to the then Mayor William Eckman, there was only one case of looting in La Plata after the tornado passed, but it was not at this particular establishment. The mayor provided me with the next photograph along with the funny note.

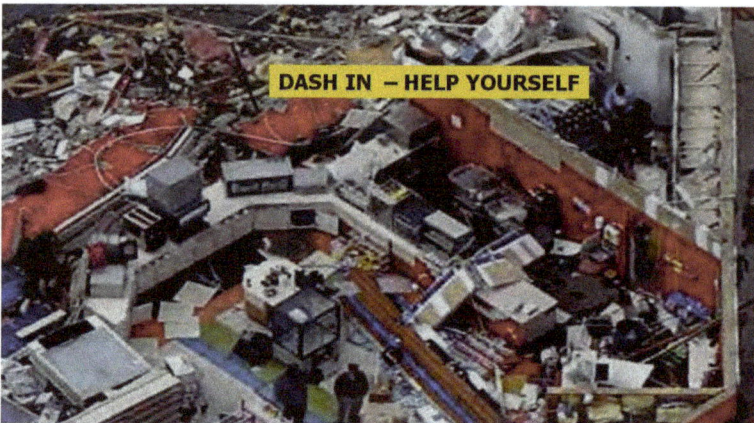

6-104: DASH IN – HELP YOURSELF.

6-105: *The Dash-In Store Entrance.*

What the employees experienced on that fateful day was captured in the Town of La Plata's **Memory Lane Exhibit** publication.

> Working and perched right in the path of the oncoming tornado, employees of the La Plata Dash In braced for the oncoming "train". They knew this train was different, not like the trains that passed the store on a daily basis. The manager Pat Frazier instructed the employees to immediately go into the bathroom, which harbored four interior walls, and closed the door, not knowing what to expect. When they emerged unharmed, the damage was extensive and the roof was gone. They were afraid as they had never been through anything like this, but were unharmed.

6-106: *The Dash-In Experience*

Falling trees damaged a number of homes on Worchester Street as the tornado finally left the downtown area of La Plata. This photograph shows the damage in the 600 block of Worchester Street.

6-107: *Damage on Worchester Street.*

The blessed and riveting story told by Pat and Fred Reitz to Victoria A. Weiss in August 2008 appeared in the latter's book A WHIRLWIND OF STORIES, La Plata Tornado, 2002.

Blessed Mother Protects Family

I live on Worcester Street in La Plata (2 blocks behind the hospital) and on April 28, 2002, my husband and I were home and we were able to get to the basement in time. We listened while all the windows and doors in our house were blown out; we had no idea what we would find when it was over.

We sustained much damage to the outside of the house and all our trees were uprooted. Both of our cars were totaled. The inside could have been a lot worse but mostly there was glass everywhere.

The story we would like to share however has to do with our spare office/computer room. When we looked into that room we saw the TV lying on the bed; it had blown off the dresser and onto the bed. All my books, CDs and other things that were on the shelves over the computer desk were scattered all over the room. There was an inch of glass on the floors because the sliding door had blown out. The only thing that was still in place after the tornado was my marble statue of the Blessed Mother. She stood in place, as though she was protecting the house and us.

We were one of the lucky ones - we were able to stay in our house because the next day volunteers from the South Potomac Church came and boarded up all our windows. We had no water, electricity, or phone for most of the week, but we were able to start clean-up (with the help of friends, relatives, and the good Amish people) and were provided with food and water by many volunteers from the American Red Cross.

The tornado did a lot of damage, but it also brought our whole neighborhood closer together. And 6 years later, we are still close - thanks to the tornado.

Pat and Fred Reitz
August 2008

6-108: *The Reitz's story.*

Two destroyed homes are shown in the following picture on Normandie Woods Drive. Seven people were inside one of these houses; all seven survived (three were in the basement, two were on the first floor headed to the basement, and two were on the second floor). A second house (in the background) also was flattened. The photograph was submitted to the Charles County Government by Warren Robinette.

6-109: *Residential Damage on Normandie Woods Drive.*

Ronnie Taylor sorts through the remains of his uncle's La Plata home on Normandie Woods Drive. The photograph was taken by Andrea Bruce Woodall for *The Washington Post*.

6-110: *Home on Normandie Woods Drive.*

As the tornado continued its eastbound trek, it struck Hawkins Gate Road. In an instant, it changed the world for Laura Silk and her family.

Laura Silk was in the dining room when she noticed the funnel cloud heading right for her La Plata home. "I see it! I see it!" she screamed, according to her husband, Steve, who helped gather the children — Steven, 11, Philip, 9, and Dana, 7. They headed for the basement.

The family members initially huddled under the stairwell, but at the last second, they moved to another area, away from the stairs. The parents grabbed a mattress and covered themselves and the children just before the impact.

"The next thing I saw was daylight, daylight where the first floor had been," said Laura Silk.

The stairwell that they had originally gone to get under cover was destroyed. The entire house had been leveled to the foundation, lopped cleanly from the bottom. All their possessions had been scattered and smashed.

But the Silk family was alive, and that's what counted. They joined their fellow neighbors on Hawkins Gate Road who lost their homes, surveying the damage under the harsh beams of fire and rescue workers' floodlights on Sunday evening.

As the Silk children huddled under blankets, Steve and Laura marveled at their fortune, which at that moment seemed to be good fortune indeed, even though they had lost nearly everything. Others were not as lucky.

STAFF PHOTO BY GARY SMITH

Laura Silk looks into the valley below her family's Hawkins Gate Road home in La Plata. Sunday's storm destroyed the home.

The Silks' neighbor, William G. Erickson Jr., 51, had died when his house, under construction nearby, was leveled by the storm. Erickson's wife, Susan, was injured. The couple was apparently looking over the house when the storm hit, according to neighbors and rescue workers.

Erickson's house, just up the street on Martha Hawkins Place, was just a few yards away from the Stapleton family, whose home was damaged but not destroyed by the storm.

"We saw it all through the basement window," said Sheila Stapleton. The storm approached slowly at first, she recalled, "Then we saw it moving. Stuff was flying."

When it was over, she and other neighbors began to check on one another. But the Ericksons' home was flattened. "We could hear some-body screaming, crying ... but we couldn't get to them," Stapleton said.

Rescue workers eventually arrived and transported Susan Erickson to a hospital, but what could have been a horror scene eventually became one of comfort and consolation, as neighbors throughout the Hawkins' Purchase subdivision stopped by to talk. They had all suffered tremendous losses.

Other homes along the end of the Hawkins Gate Road cul-de-sac were damaged. Windows had been blown out. Siding had been peeled away. Roofs had been sheared off. Another home that had just been completed, ready for final inspection, was now in pieces.

6-111: *Horror on Hawkins Gate Road.*

This photograph was taken looking down at the end of Hawkins Gate Road. According to Tim Marshall, with Haag Engineering, there appeared to be two vortex paths. One spared the house on the lower left. This path moved through the trees just north of the house. The other vortex struck the house on the center right of the picture and continued its F3 destruction of residential homes before entering the woods. This image was adapted from Google Maps.

6-112: *Two vortex paths down Hawkins Gate Road.*

On the 28th day of April, 2002, at the Jameson Manor Farm, located at 7061 Olivers Shop Road near Hughesville, Maryland, it was a beautiful, sunny day. Then hell broke loose for the family of Robert and Alicia Stahl. Here is their story as told to Nancy Bromley McConaty, a staff writer for the *Maryland Independent*. Her article, "Family counts blessings after storm rips Jameson Manor," appeared in the Friday, May 3, 2002, edition of the newspaper.

Robert and Alicia Stahl and their two small children barely made it into the basement of their Bryantown home before Sunday's powerful tornado plowed through a field and slammed into their house.

The twister ripped the third floor and both porches completely off Jameson Manor, shattered all of the windows and destroyed a large cattle barn.

Before the tornado hit it was a typical Sunday evening for the couple. Stahl's parents, Jean and Robert, were visiting for dinner. Alicia and her mother-in-law were in the kitchen preparing the meal when she glanced out of the window and saw storm clouds gathering around their house on Olivers Shop Road.

"I saw it coming through the woods, and I said to my mother, 'Come take a look at this,'" she said, while standing Wednesday in shattered glass and other debris in one of the house's destroyed rooms. "I couldn't tell if it was a tornado. I didn't see a funnel. There was this huge, black grayish cloud."

Robert Stahl said he looked outside and knew right away a tornado was barreling toward their house.

"I saw it coming," he said. "Alicia was cooking dinner. My parents were here. She said, 'Bobby, look how bad the storm looks.' I said, 'That's not a storm. That's a tornado, and it's coming right toward us. Let's get down to the basement.'

"I watched it about two minutes, and I saw it hit the woods. It was unbelievable. I saw the trees go right up into the air."

The family quickly scrambled downstairs to the basement to wait out the storm.

"I ducked down to cover Alicia and the kids up," Stahl said, "It was no more than a minute or two. I heard a deafening roar. Then all of a sudden, dead silence."

When the family emerged from the basement Stahl went outside to survey the damage. The third floor of the house was sheared off from the force of the wind. Both porches were ripped off the house.

The chimney crashed through the roof and into the Stahl's newly renovated kitchen.

The roof and one wall of their son's bedroom caved in, leaving large chunks of debris piled on top of his bed.

"If he had been in the room when the tornado hit he would have been killed," Alicia said.

Stahl's pickup, Alicia's car and his parents' vehicle were destroyed.

"My truck hit the house but I never heard it," he said.

"I didn't hear the truck hit the house. I didn't hear the chimney hit the house. I didn't hear everything being ripped apart," Alicia said. "That we just walked away amazes me."

Stahl raises Black Angus cattle. Six of the 17 animals were trapped in what was left of a large barn behind the house.

"They were trapped under the rubble. They were smashed flat," he said. "Their legs were buckled beneath them. It took us three to four hours to get them out."

Fortunately, the animals were not injured.

"They're a little skittish around the barn, though," he said.

The couple's children, Robert III, 6, and Lizzy, 9, survived the storm unscathed, Alicia said.

"There's not a scratch on any of us," she said. "I just can't believe it. When we were in the basement the children were screaming. They were so scared, especially my daughter. She's 9 and she knew what was going on. She keeps asking me, 'Why did this happen to us?'"

Lizzy is very upset because a barn cat the family has adopted is missing, her mother said.

"She keeps asking if we've found Kit-Kat," she said.

The county has condemned the house, Stahl said, but the couple plans to rebuild. The family is staying in a friend's recreational vehicle, but Stahl said they will be temporarily moving into a rental house within the next week.

Another friend gave the couple a car to use, and Frank Chaney of Chaney Enterprises loaned Stahl a pickup until his vehicle can be replaced.

PHOTO BY FAYE STINEHART LITTLE

Family members look for livestock after Sunday's tornado collapsed a barn at Jameson Manor near Hughesville.

6-113: *Jameson Farm Manor near Hughesville.*

This aerial view of the Jameson Farm Manor shows the eerie scene after the passage of the tornado. This photograph was submitted to the Charles County Government by Warren Robinette.

6-114: *Jameson Farm Manor.*

The tornado continued to head east, spewing destruction to Hughesville and Benedict and across the Putuxent River into Calvert County.

A barn on Steve Walter's devastated five-hundred-eighty-acre farm in Hughesville lied in rubble after the passage of the tornado. "We're wiped out," Walter lamented after viewing the destruction.

6-115: Farm in Hughesville.

On Homeland Drive in Hughesville, a van was tumbled and smashed. This photograph was taken by Anita Drury for the *Maryland Independent* newspaper.

6-116: Overturned Van in Hughesville.

The *Maryland Independent*, published on Wednesday, October 9, 2002, related this story written by John Yellig, a staff writer with the newspaper: "Bent and broken trees behind an empty lot greet visitors to Homeland Drive in Hughesville, a short street that suffered some of the most concentrated destruction outside La Plata. Farther down the block, a capped-off water main and a concrete pallet are all that remain of a house that was erased by the storm. Michael D. Grigley Jr., a contractor, was one of the homelanders who were hit hardest. He was watching golf with his parents on April 28, 2002, when his father noticed the house vibrating. "He told us to get downstairs," he said. "Not three seconds later after we got there, the tornado ripped apart my house. What the tornado didn't take down, I had to tear down," he said.

The American Flag flies from a storm-ravaged house off of Route 231 in Hughesville.

6-117: *The American Flag still flies in Hughesville.*

Patty Williams, who lives in Hughesville, related her story which appeared in the publication A *Whirlwind of Stories*, La Plata Tornado, 2002, to Victoria A. Weiss in August 2008.

The Sky Turned Black

We live in Hughesville, Maryland along the tornado's path. The afternoon was pleasant here, comfortable and I had opened the windows to let in the spring air. My husband was recovering from chemotherapy and radiation treatments. He had gotten thin and weak and our 3 children came for a visit that day. To cheer their dad up, the kids drove their dad to the Bass Pro Shop to buy him some 'toys': a small BB gun and paper targets along with some new fishing gear. With the whole family away for the afternoon, I prepared a big supper and readied the house for a celebration. This was the first time in a year we had all the kids home at once. Our oldest daughter was stationed in Louisiana in the Air Force and her visit was especially welcomed. My mother came and about 6:30, the shoppers returned. As they unwrapped packages, one of our daughters asked, "Hey, Mom, did you hear we have a tornado warning?" I had been listening to music on a CD and hadn't heard any news. I've lived in Charles County most of my life and didn't remember having a tornado here, so I didn't worry. I glanced outside, the evening looked beautiful to me and I thought, "Gee, I don't see any signs of a storm." A few minutes later as I set a big pan of lasagna on the dinner table, I glanced outside and noticed the wind picking up, so I closed the windows. My son came in and said he put our trash cans in the garage. I said, "That's nice dear. Now sit down so we can eat before dinner gets cold."

We bowed our heads and started to say grace and heard loud rumbling and the sky turned black. Still not taking the tornado threat too seriously, I ended our prayer with, "And please God, let the tornado blow over our house." Just then, through the windows we saw trees in the backyard blowing and bent to the south. When we looked out front, trees blew in the opposite direction. The rumble got so loud we couldn't hear each other so everyone stopped talking and just watched as the wind whipped branches and debris through the air. It rained hard for a few, maybe two or three minutes and then, in just as quickly, everything calmed. There was rain but not nearly as hard as a moment ago. Two of my kids ran outside to get some hail balls. I hollered at them and when they returned, the hail they carried was the size of baseballs.

We put the hail in the freezer and since the storm had passed, we sat back down to eat dinner by candle light. A half hour later, we heard the sounds of chainsaws in the distance. We thought some trees must be down. Well, we thought, that's not surprising; it was a pretty strong wind.

For the next two hours, we visited, unaware of how intense the storm had been. Around nine p.m., my mother said good night and left. A few minutes later, she returned and said there were trees all over the road and houses torn up along our street. Our family members checked with neighbors to see if anyone was hurt or needed help. Fortunately, everyone on our street was unharmed. Only a few of the buildings were damaged. Some of the homes nearby were hit hard, some had roofing torn away, windows broken and siding blown off. The hardest hit was the minister's home on 231. Luckily, no one was home but the house was a mess. The kids took flashlights and saws and went to see if they could help anyone.

6-118: Patty's Story.

Here are some of the baseball hailstones which fell in Hughesville, as described by Patty Williams in her interview.

6-119: Hailstones in Hughesville.

There were a total of seven-hundred and thirty-eight homes damaged in Hughesville due to the passing of the tornado. Before crossing the Patuxent River and entering Calvert County, the tornado passed just below Benedict at Golden Beach.

The home of Carolyn and Dick Magill was opened and exposed as if it were a doll house.

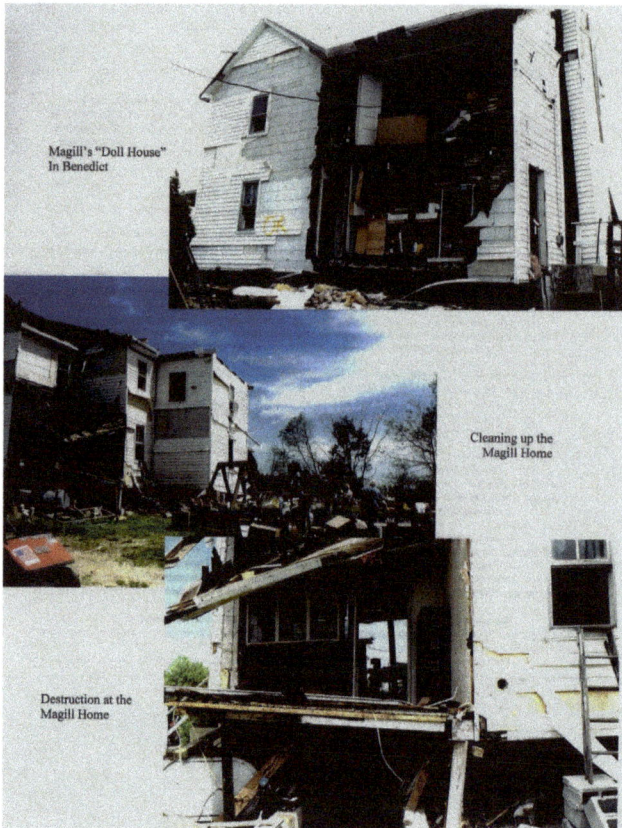

Magill's "Doll House" In Benedict

Cleaning up the Magill Home

Destruction at the Magill Home

6-120: *The Destruction of the Magill House*

Carolyn's horrid story was told to Victoria Weiss in September 2008, for the latter's publication, A WHIRLWIND OF STORIES, La Plata Tornado, 2002.

Son's Phone Call Saves Family

We had just had a turkey dinner. My husband Dick, daughter Brenda Debusk, and brother-in-law Ronnie Magill were over for dinner. It was a great day. All of a sudden it was humid. My son, Rick, called me and said I had to get out of the house. He said that a tornado was coming. To get to our basement, you had to go outside the house and around the back. We looked out the windows and my husband said that things weren't looking good. I saw the green skies, which is when all the leaves are in the air. The tornado was coming faster than we could run. My husband said to run and get in the basement so we all took off running for the basement. I didn't hear the train but everyone else I was with said they heard it. I was so focused on getting into the basement that I wasn't paying attention to anything else.

We got into the basement and tried to shut the door. The four of us were leaning against the door, trying to keep it closed but we were thrown. My husband went to the right and the door landed on top of him, which saved him. My daughter, brother-in-law, and I went to the left. My brother-in-law pushed my daughter into the corner, pushed himself against her, grabbed me by the waist, and he held onto a pole. I could see everything coming in the door. I tried to hold onto my yellow lab, Gus, who was about 120 pounds, but I couldn't and he went out the window.

When it was all over it made a suction in the house. The house lifted and moved us. My brother-in-law had to let go of me and then I floated in the air. I thought I was dead. It was kind of a cool feeling because I was weightless and I was just hanging there. Then all of a sudden, it slowly put me down, my hands touched the furnace, and it was all over. It all happened within seconds. We barely had enough time to get in the basement before it hit.

When we came up out of the basement, it was like someone had picked us up and put us somewhere else. We didn't know where we were. It looked like everything had been sucked out of the ground; trees, roots and all were gone. One side of our house looked like a dollhouse because it was completely open. We just stood there in a daze. If we had stayed in the kitchen, we would have been gone because that side of the house was completely open. Our dog, Gus, met us at the basement door. He was barking and looking up in the sky like he knew there was something there. Gus was about 3 or 4 years old at the time, and to this day he is still afraid of storms.

I recall my first instinct when we were running around the house toward the basement, was to jump into my van but my brother-in-law yelled at me not to get in there. When we came out of the basement, I looked at my van and realized that if I had been in there I would have been dead. All the windows were blown out and it was severely damaged. I told my husband that I thought his deceased grandmother and grandfather were there looking out for us because when I looked into my van, there was a picture of them sitting on the seat. The picture came out of the house and somehow made its way into my van. It was the only picture that I found outside the house. When we went back inside the house, the turkey that we had been eating was still sitting in exactly the same spot. There wasn't even any debris or anything on it. It was incredible.

People were so giving; so many people came and helped us clean up after the tornado. We were so thankful for that. For years after the tornado, my two neighbors and I used to get together for dinner at someone's house and we would talk about our experiences with the tornado. I guess it helped us to talk about what happened. It made the whole ordeal easier.

Carolyn Magill
As told to Victoria Weiss
September 2008

6-121: *Carolyn's story.*

Marty Jordan, and his wife, Michelle, had spent six years fixing up their Benedict home. The tornado destroyed it in seconds.

6-122: *The Jordan's Benedict home.*

The tornado entered Calvert County south of the Patuxent River Bridge (Route 231) at 7:28 p.m. EDT, after traversing thirty miles. Although it was weakening, it still was strong enough to destroy several homes and kill two people in Calvert County. The tornado damage in Calvert County was rated F1 to F2 intensity.

Homes in Calvert County suffered predominantly roof and siding damage. The occupants of the home shown below had safely taken cover in an interior bathroom. This photograph was taken by Ed Pae, N3HJA, Skywarn volunteer for NWS and a HAM operator.

6-123: Damaged home in Calvert County.

Rick Hilmer was nice enough to send me the following information regarding the tornado's movement and activity once it entered Calvert County.

> *We live in Long Beach in Calvert County over on the bay. The tornado exited Calvert County and crossed the bay a quarter to a half mile from our house. We were paying attention to the reports (did not have cell phone apps and such like today) on the TV and radio and we knew it was coming right at us. At the critical time my wife, kids, dog and I all crowded into the laundry room*

(no basement!) as it was the main option for an interior room. There was a vent in the bottom of the door that allowed the furnace to breathe, and at the time that the tornado went by we experienced the drop in pressure and witnessed the air rush out of the laundry room through the door vent. It was something, and we intuitively knew exactly what it meant.

We did not have any damage at our house, but did not have to go far to find the swath that it cut through the trees on its way through the area.

The tornado exited Calvert County near Long Beach at 7:45 p.m. and entered the Chesapeake Bay. The following picture shows damage to a swath of trees along the shoreline. It was taken by the Calvert County Office of Emergency Management.

6-124: Shoreline Damage in Long Beach.

Additional F1 and F0 tornado damage, mostly in the form of downed trees, would continue in Dorchester and Wicomico Counties across the Chesapeake Bay.

I will end this particular chapter with signs of hope within the Town of La Plata, despite the turmoil and despair the tornado inflicted on the populace and their property.

The first photograph shows CVS employees selling items on folding tables, just outside their heavily damaged store in La Plata.

6-125: *CVS still operating.*

The next photograph shows the marquee outside Martin's gas station, expressing a positive note.

6-126: "WE WILL REBUILD."

The residents of this Oak Avenue home in La Plata send a message after the tornado strikes. "We'll be Back." Dallas Cogle, a staff photographer with the *Maryland Independent*, took the photograph.

6-127: "We'll be Back."

CHAPTER 7

The Response to the Disaster

In the preparation of this chapter, I received invaluable assistance from three people. First, and foremost, William Eckman, who was the Mayor of La Plata at the time and was highly instrumental not only the immediate response to the disaster, but also in the planning and implementation of the long-term recovery and restoration of the town following the tornado. Most of the material, photographs, and images used in this chapter were generously provided by him. I also received assistance from William Daniel Mayer, who was the County Commissioner for District 1 (La Plata) at the time of the tornado, and Donna Thomas, who was a Red Cross volunteer in La Plata during the tornado. Both provided photographs and contemporary newspapers and other material used in this chapter.

Mayor Eckman summarized the Town's ability to respond to this terrible disaster so quickly and decisively. "The one outstanding thing that made the recovery possible was all the help the Town received. Twenty-Seven different jurisdictions sent help in the form of vehicles, heavy equipment and the personnel to operate them. In particular, the cities of Washington D.C. and Baltimore, Maryland, came through big time. D.C had people on the scene in La Plata by Tuesday, and their delegation eventually included nearly one-hundred-and-fifty people. They sent a mobile command post and one of their emergency management supervisors to help coordinate the cleanup. Their delegation even included a battalion chief from the fire department to serve as safety officer. Baltimore sent seventeen trucks, several pieces of heavy equipment and thirty-five men to operate them. The Governor and many of the state agencies participated in the recovery. They were all there when they were needed and they continued to stay with us during the rebuilding of the Town. During the second week when the major cleanup took place, there were three-hundred pieces of equipment and six-hundred workers in Town including twenty-five percent of the total resources of the Maryland State Highway Administration."

In addition, the Amish and Mennonites from St. Mary's County played a vital role in cutting and clearing the literally tons of trees which fell all over Charles and Calvert Counties. The Mayor said, "God Bless them. The Amish don't talk; they just work."

Even though most of the property damage occurred within the Town of La Plata, this tornado stayed on the ground for thirty-eight miles.

Within the boundaries of the Town, the entire basic infrastructure was destroyed.

When the water tank was destroyed, the Town's water system was drained and there was no water in the fire hydrants. The capacity of the water tank that was destroyed was only seventy-five-thousand gallons of water and the system had two other tanks that still had more than one million gallons in storage. Unfortunately, when the tank was destroyed by the tornado, the riser was broken at ground level. The entire one million gallons stored in the other elevated tanks escaped through the broken pipe and drained the system within minutes of the time the tornado hit. Many water pipes were broken when buildings were destroyed. When the water pressure was restored, the Town Public Works Crews had to turn off the individual cutoff valves to prevent further loss from the system. One difficulty was the fact that the destruction was so complete that the maintenance crews had trouble finding where the shutoff valves were located. The Town had three major production wells in service at the time of the tornado. Normally, they would run to refill the system after it was drained. However, although one of the wells had an emergency generator, it didn't start. Although none of the wells were physically damaged, the electricity was lost to all of them and none of the pumps would run to refill them.

7-1: *The water tower.*

Fortunately, there were no fires during the entire incident, even though the cleanup operation took many days to complete. As the tornado went through, the electric lines were destroyed, so there was no electricity anywhere in the damaged area, effectively impeding the restoration of the water system, telecommunications, and other critical infrastructures.

7-2: *Electrical poles down.*

In addition, there was no communication available within the Town of La Plata due to damage to equipment and the lack of electricity. All of the telephone cables, cable TV and electric lines in the damaged area were totally destroyed. All the regular telephone service was out, and cell phone towers were overloaded. In addition to the lack of service, demand was heavy as homeowners tried in vain to check on their property, and the people they knew who resided in the Town.

7-3: Telecommunication infrastructure destroyed.

The following organizational chart was established in order to address La Plata's recovery operations. Their operational locations are denoted on the chart.

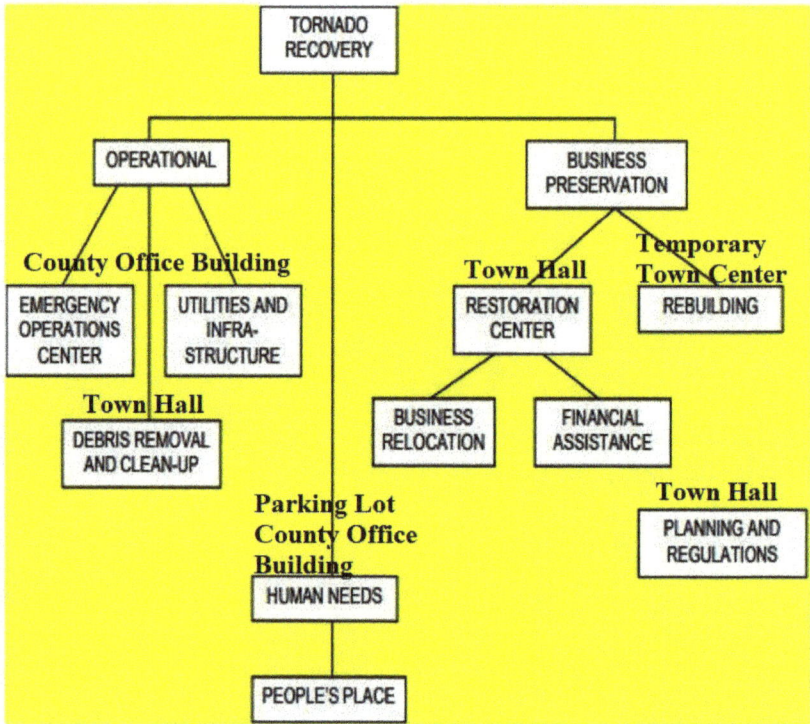

7-4: *Organization chart.*

INITIAL RESPONSE – SEARCH AND RESCUE.

During any emergency, such as this when collapsed buildings and debris trap victims underneath, the first order of business is to find and rescue people as soon as possible and transport them to medical facilities and first aid stations. There was property damage spread out from the village of Ripley west of La Plata to the Patuxent River on the eastern boundary of Charles County. Emergency services units were responding to calls all over the County. Damage was also widespread in Calvert County, and the St. Mary's County units were called on to assist from the very start of the incident.

An Emergency Operations Center (EOC) was needed to co-ordinate the search and rescue operation. An EOC was set up in the cafeteria of the County office building, and the supervisor at the 911 center agreed to take charge of the Center. Police, fire, and emergency medical activities were directed from this EOC all during the clean-up and recovery effort.The Emergency Management Director from Ocean City, Maryland, arrived on the Monday morning following the disaster (April 29th). He immediately worked with Charles County Emergency Management personnel in setting up the EOC and getting it in operation.

The Charles County Rescue Squad (LPTD 16) at 2 Calvert Street was unfortunately limited in its response to the disaster.

7-5: *The Charles County Rescue Squad building.*

The Charles County Rescue Squad (CCRS) building, where the first due ambulances were housed, was damaged by the tornado. Even more important, access to the building was blocked by debris. It was some time until ambulances could get out of the building to treat and transport the injured. By a stroke of good fortune, one of the Rescue Squad BLS units was on Route 301 several miles north of La Plata returning from a call in Waldorf when the tornado went through. This ambulance responded immediately to the intersection of Routes 301 and 6 where many of the injured were concentrated. A number of mutual aid ambulances from other local area rescue stations (Bel Alton and Bryans Road) also responded immediately, and they were able to care for the injured in a timely manner.

An emergency command post was set up in the parking lot of the Charles County government building in La Plata. The building faces Baltimore Street, and is behind the soccer field (see the La Plata's Tornado Damage Map). A Chief Officer from the La Plata Fire Department was the incident commander and assumed responsibility for directing the search and rescue operation. The initial search took place immediately. It was followed by a more detailed search and rescue effort. The D.C. Fire and EMS Cave-in Task Force arrived at 11 p.m. and assisted in the search and rescue operation throughout the night. A final search covering the same territory took place on Monday morning after daylight to verify that no buried victim had been overlooked. Rescue workers were gratified to find that no one was trapped in the debris.

7-6: Search and rescue operations.

D.C. Fire and EMS Helps La Plata Recover From Tornado Disaster

DC.gov website, Fire and EMS Department, dated Wednesday, May 8, 2002.

Nearly two weeks after a deadly tornado touched down in the seat of Charles County, Maryland, D.C. Fire/ EMS experts remained on the scene helping officials maintain safe operations around the disaster sites.

Two hours after the F-4 tornado ripped through the community on April 28th, D.C. units were rolling to the scene. A Cave-In Task Force, under the direction of Bat-

*talion Fire Chief Phil Pestone, was dispatched to aug-
ment county and state rescue teams already on the ground.
D.C. Fire/EMS personnel conducted searches of scores of
collapsed buildings in conditions one official likened to
"a war zone."*

7-7: Washington, D.C. Rescue Squad truck.

A western triage area was established in the parking lot of the Safeway
store at the intersection of Crain Highway and Charles Street. An eastern
site was set up in front of the Port Tobacco Theater on Charles Street.
The Medstar helicopter was deployed and was stationed at the western
triage site.

7-8: *The Medstar helicopter.*

The various emergency medical units performed first aid and transported the injured to the hospital for treatment. No serious injuries were reported, but more than two-hundred patients were treated at Civista Medical Center for various injuries. While there was some minor damage to the hospital and nearby (broken windows and damage to vehicles in the parking lot), the hospital remained fully functional throughout the incident. As the storm approached, patients were quickly moved to safety and a remote triage area was set up in anticipation of multiple casualties. After the tornado hit, patients started arriving by foot and in the back of pick-up trucks, as well as by ambulance. On the day of the tornado, Tony Ross, the Deputy Director of the Charles County Department of Emergency Services, recalls driving on Charles Street and seeing scores of injured people staggering towards the hospital, seeking medical aid. The hospital was soon overwhelmed with patients, but the staff rose to the occasion and handled the situation superbly.

7-9: *Civista Hospital.*

INITIAL RESPONSE – TRAFFIC CONTROL AND ACCESS TO THE AREA BY EMERGENCY VEHICLES AND SECURTY ISSUES.

The La Plata Police Department, the Charles County Sheriff's Department (CCSD), and the Maryland State Police (MSP) responded immediately in addressing the dual issues of traffic control and security. Their first concern was controlling traffic and providing full access to the area for emergency vehicles, despite the massive influx of curious motorists.

7-10: *Traffic control.*

Security was a secondary concern, both to prevent looting and to control access to keep bystanders and residents of the damaged buildings from being injured. It was especially important to prevent anyone from entering damaged buildings that might be in danger of collapsing.

7-11: Security control.

Within fifteen minutes of the time the tornado went through the Town, representatives from all types of emergency service agencies arrived at the command post and began to get it organized. All mutual aid units reported to the command post when they arrived and received their assignments from the incident commander. A number of mobile command posts were also there within a short time. The Charles County Sheriff's mobile command post unit was positioned at the command post in the parking lot, and handled communication with all emergency units responding throughout the area, as well as on the scene.

7-12: *The Charles County Sheriff's mobile command post.*

The Maryland State Police and State Highway mobile command units soon arrived as well. Local government officials arrived at the command post within minutes of the time the tornado went through Town. All contact with the media took place at the command post, and all of the different agencies were represented there. Representatives from the State Highway Administration (SHA), including the Secretary of Transportation, Maryland State Police, and other state agencies, arrived at the command post within the hour, ready to do whatever had to bedone to cope with the emergency situation. Here is the Maryland State Police helicopter departing on one of its multiple missions.

7-13: *Maryland State Police helicopter.*

IMMEDIATE ACTION
CARING FOR THE DISPLACED AND
FEEDING – RED CROSS AND OTHERS.

Once the search and rescue operation was underway and the damaged areas were secured, there were a number of immediate needs that had to be addressed. First and most important was to take care of the injured and homeless. The Charles County Chapter of the Red Cross, with the strong support of the National Chapter, responded immediately and began to provide for those in need. An emergency shelter was set up at the Thomas Stone High School in Waldorf and arrangements made to care for the residents who had lost everything when the tornado destroyed their homes. In addition, the Red Cross established a temporary emergency shelter at the Judicial Services Center behind the District 1 station of the Charles County Sheriff's Office at 6845 Crain Highway in La Plata.

In Calvert County, the Red Cross said four homes were destroyed, three had moderate damage and sixteen homes sustained minor damage. The Red Cross helped eleven families find motel rooms.

Emergency services personnel worked through the night and needed sustenance. Several of the local restaurants provided food and drinks at the command post. A number of golf carts made their appearance and several of the local service groups traveled throughout the damaged area, delivering food and drinks to the rescue workers and people that were helping to clear enough debris to make the streets and roads passable. This service continued through the two weeks of the cleanup and recovery. The Red Cross brought in six of their mobile canteens, some from Virginia, West Virginia, and other locations some distance away from La Plata. They provided food and drinks as they traveled throughout the area that was destroyed by the tornado.

7-14: *Red Cross canteen.*

Before we continue with this particular discussion, we need to be cognizant of the fact that during this entire time helping and feeding others, the American Red Cross, Charles County Chapter in La Plata was undergoing its own trauma and internal problems. Its own facility, located at the Norris Building II (LPTD 41), was heavily damaged by the tornado.

7-15: *The damaged Red Cross facility in La Plata.*

This Chapter, with the help and assistance of other volunteers from neighboring chapters, set up a disaster Command Post in the parking lot of the other Charles County Government Center. Donna Thomas and Debra Storey, volunteers with the Charles County Chapter of the Red Cross, are seen in front of their Mobile Service Center unit located at the command post.

7-16: *The American Red Cross Mobile Service Center.*

During the next two days, the Charles County Chapter were able to amass four-hundred-thirty volunteers from Maryland, Delaware, and across the country, eighty-one Red Cross vehicles, including ten mobile feeding units and spent nearly $200,000 in direct assistance to victims. **What a tremendous effort on the part of the Charles County Chapter in the face of their own challenges and tribulations.**

An account of the Red Cross efforts was related by Sara K. Taylor, a Staff Writer, for the *Maryland Independent*. The article entitled, "Red Cross offers victims shelter from the storm," appeared in the Wednesday, May 1, 2002, Special Edition of the newspaper.

The temporary shelter at Stone in Waldorf housed about 30 people displaced by Sunday's tornado. Ironically, the Charles County chapter of the American Red Cross building in La Plata was leveled and the volunteers that were tending to the victims at Stone are not sure what will happen next.

"Our chapter house has been destroyed," said Mike Miller, a disaster relief worker with the Red Cross of Charles County. "All we had when we started last night was literally this," he said holding up one tablet of paper and a pen.

But they were ready.

"Within a couple of hours we had staging areas set up," Miller said. "A bathroom and a roof over their heads until we could get them here [at Stone]."

Help came from the Montgomery, Prince George's and national chapters of the Red Cross, as well, Miller said.

The shelter received victims who were transported by bus or the few who could make it by car, while hospitals admitted at least a hundred patients for care.

Stone was equipped with nurses' stations and makeshift health offices in the school's guidance offices for those suffering from minor injuries.

Where school counselors normally sit, tornado victims phoned to check on their families, and volunteers took calls from area businesses looking to help.

"We've had some major contributors that have really helped out," said Karen Maguire, a disaster relief volunteer with the Red Cross. "Checkers, BoJangles, I-HOP, Old Country Buffet, Snow Valley Water Co., the Food Lion on [Route] 925, [and] the [Leonardtown Road] 7-11 have stepped up."

7-17: The Red Cross in action.

One of the families that was forced to seek shelter with the Red Cross at the Thomas Stone High School in Waldorf was the Barnes family. The tornado had gutted their townhouse. The roof over their second floor was gone and the family's belongings were scattered. The family took shelter from the tornado in their basement. Until they could find temporary lodging at the Econolodge in Waldorf, they had to settle on sleeping on cots in the gymnasium of the high school.

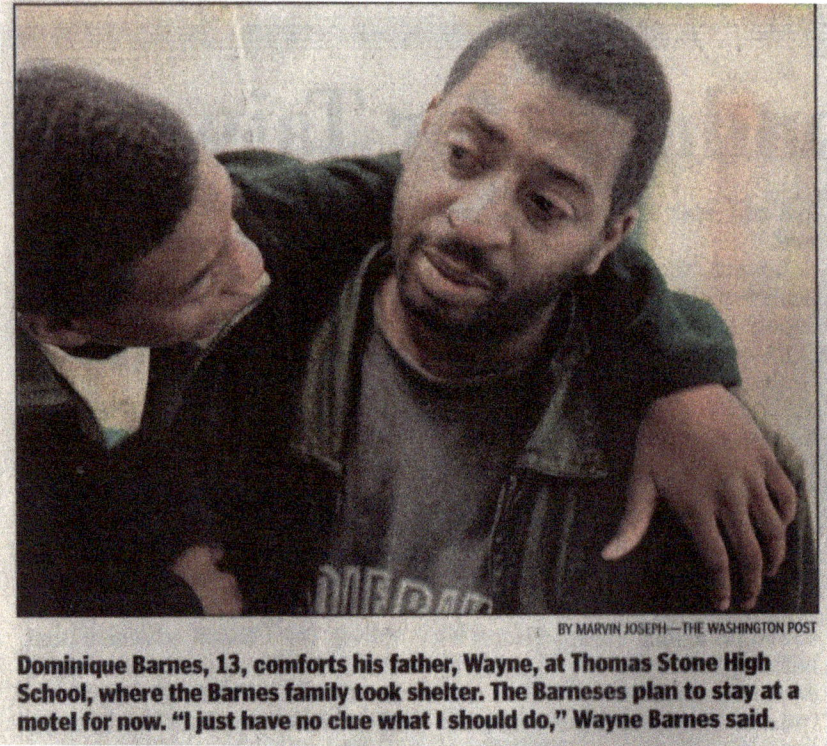

BY MARVIN JOSEPH—THE WASHINGTON POST

Dominique Barnes, 13, comforts his father, Wayne, at Thomas Stone High School, where the Barnes family took shelter. The Barneses plan to stay at a motel for now. "I just have no clue what I should do," Wayne Barnes said.

7-18: The Barnes' family trauma.

Continuing with our discussion, a mobile canteen from a church group on the Eastern Shore of Maryland set up in a trailer at the intersection of Oak Avenue and Worcester Street, and provided three meals a day for the entire neighborhood while the power was out. The disaster response trailer from the Eastern Baptist Association was used to feed three-thousand meals, a like number of snacks, and many times over soft drinks and bottled water. This unit continued to feed the neighborhood and emergency workers for two weeks while the major cleanup was taking place. All of this was done as a service to the community without any charge for anything that was provided. Bless them.

Volunteers with the Eastern Baptist Association Disaster Relief Team are seen working along Oak Street in La Plata. Dallas Cogle of the *Maryland Independent* took this photograph.

7-19: The Eastern Baptist Association relief team.

In addition, the Salvation Army provided an Emergency Disaster Services (EDS) van with food and other basic necessities. In the first week after the tornado, the Salvation Army served five thousand, three-hundred thirty-eight meals. The organization set up eight canteens in the hardest-hit residential neighborhoods and the business section of La Plata in order to serve meals to workers. Counselors from the Salvation Army and FEMA were also provided to offer mental therapy to those who lost property in the disaster.

7-20: *Salvation Army EDS Van.*

Another positive aspect in the recovery effort was aid from the community itself. The damaged Safeway grocery store donated food for the volunteers, as did local pizza restaurants and the Outback Steakhouse. One volunteer said he had never been fed so well during a disaster. Fuel, generators, and golf carts (which made traveling around the debris much easier than larger vehicles) were also donated by various paternal organizations and local businesses.

BEGINNING THE CLEANUP

As earlier mentioned, the Mayor of Ocean City, Maryland, and his Director of Emergency Management arrived on Monday and were instrumental in helping to get the cleanup and recovery organized without any delay. An Emergency Operations Center was set up in the Town Hall at 5 Garrett Avenue in order to coordinate the cleanup. The Town Hall was damaged and sections of the roof were torn off by the storm, but the building was habitable and safe for occupancy. There was no electricity at the Town Hall and it was discovered that the Town's telephone system and the radio base station both required electricity to work. The Town Hall did not have an emergency generator and a portable generator was brought in the next day to get the communications system operational and to provide lighting. The following photograph of the La Plata Town

Hall was generously provided courtesy of *Maryland Manual On-Line*, Maryland State Archives.

7-21: *The La Plata Town Hall.*

This Center was operated on a day-to-day basis under the supervision of the safety director from Ocean City. He was a trained and experienced incident commander and had been involved in previous natural disasters. The Town was divided into five zones and each crew was assigned to one of them when they reported in. As relief crews arrived from other jurisdictions, they reported to the Town Hall and the cleanup effort was managed from this center.

The full extent of the damage wasn't obvious until daylight broke the morning following the passage of the tornado. Most of the streets in the downtown were clogged with trees and debris, and were not passable. It was some time before anything more than a skeleton force was available since nearly all of the Town's public works employees and the Maryland Environmental Service employees lived outside of Town. The recovery effort really couldn't get started until the streets and roads were made usable for the trucks and heavy equipment that would be required to handle the debris. The worst damage occurred in and around the Town. The Town agreed to coordinate this phase of the cleanup in that area while the County would work with State Highway crews to begin cleaning up in the remainder of the County. The Town Manager assumed responsibility for organizing and supervising this effort in and around La Plata.

The view on Maple Avenue was typical of the problems that faced the Town on Monday morning with literally a forest of downed trees everywhere in sight.

7-22: *Maple trees on Maple Avenue.*

Town officials met with the County Commissioners and reached agreement as to the best way to approach the cleanup. The County agreed to begin disposing of the debris at the Charles County Landfill located on Billingsley Road in Waldorf, Maryland.

7-23: *The Charles County Landfill.*

The Town set up a temporary burn site on Radio Station Road until some long-term arrangements could be made. A second burn site was established on Rosewick Road in a gravel pit. The wooden waste was disposed of by using chippers and converting it to mulch. Stumps and household debris would have to be taken to a rubble landfill, but all of these were some distance from Charles County. The massive amount of debris left in the wake of the tornado sent officials scrambling to find a place to temporarily store the stuff until it was sorted and transported to appropriate landfills. The county and the Maryland Department of the Environment struck an agreement that allowed for the temporary storage of the tornado-related debris on state-owned property at the intersection of Turkey Hill Road and Route 301 north of La Plata.

7-24: *The burn site and transfer station.*

Workers used heavy equipment to move thousands of tons of debris at the temporary disposal site. The photograph was taken by James M. Thresher of *The Washington Post.*

7-25: *Heavy equipment moves mountain of debris.*

In order to collect and dispose of this mountain of debris, trees, shrubs and rubble, estimated at over twenty-five thousand tons, from the downtown area of La Plata and in the rest of Charles County, a literal army of resources were called upon or just frankly showed up like "Angels from Heaven."

The Maryland Department of Transportation, State Highway Administration (SHA), La Plata Shop provided tireless hours of effort in the removal of debris following the tornado. One week after the tornado went through, three hundred pieces of equipment and six hundred workers began the cleanup. Everything went as planned and more than ninety percent of the debris had been removed from the downtown by Noon on Friday of that week.

7-26: *The SHA crew.*

SHA crews at work in Quailwood subdivision removing debris at Quail Lane and Bob White Court.

7-27: **SHA crew at work in Quailwood.**

The City of Baltimore showed up one morning, soon after the passage of the tornado, with a convoy of trucks seen here driving up Garrett Avenue towards the Town Hall in order to join in the debris removal phase of the recovery.

7-28: *The arrival of the City of Baltimore truck convoy.*

Was the Mayor William F. Eckman, wearing a plait shirt, glad to see their arrival? Yes indeed! He was elated in April 2002, and when I met this fine and gracious gentleman in August 2021.

7-29: *The Mayor with one of the City of Baltimore crews.*

Hordes of Gradall excavation and Asplundh tree removal trucks were found everywhere after the disaster, assisting Verizon and SMECO (Southern Maryland Electric Cooperative) in the replacement of poles for telephone and electric power service.

7-30: *Gradall evacuation truck at work.*

7-31: Asplundh evacuation truck at work.

This photograph shows a utility truck loading branches into a dump truck, which were destined for the sanitary landfill.

7-32: Utility truck loading branches.

Pepco (Potomac Electric Power Company) provided assistance to SMECO as part of a mutual assistance agreement between the respective southern Maryland and Washington, D.C. and Maryland suburban-based utilities.

7-33: *Pepco crew at work repairing electrical lines.*

7-34: *Pepco truck hauling new utility poles.*

SMC Utility Networking located in Tracy's Landing, Maryland, provided utility trucks and crew to SMECO in compliance with its mutual aid agreement with the electric utility company.

7-35: SMC utility truck on-site.

In this photograph, various utility crews are seen repairing power lines along Route 6.

7-36: Utility crews at work along Route 6.

The tornado's thirty-eight mile rampage through Charles and Calvert Counties left nearly thirty-thousand customers without power in their southern Maryland service area, according to the Southern Maryland Electric Cooperative (SMECO) on Sunday night April 28th. Electric power was immediately shut off after the storm passed as downed "live" electrical wires were strewn along Route 301 and Charles Street (Route 6) and alongside streets everywhere. SMECO acted quickly to restore power, with one-hundred thirty SMECO and contract crews laboring in shifts around the clock. SMECO restored service to twenty-five-thousand customers within hours after the passage of the tornado and within three days to the remaining five thousand customers. Damage to Co-op equipment was staggering. The COOP had to repair or replace one-hundred fity-one utility poles, two-hundred twenty-five cross-arm braces, eighty-three transformers, hundreds of fuses, and many thousands of feet of conductor and guy wire. Although the tornado inflicted approximately $1.5 million of damage to SMECO's facilities, with a large concentration in the La Plata area, the Maryland Emergency Management Agency, with the assistance of the Federal Emergency Management Agency, funded most of SMECO's restoration costs. One major issue which happened, once the commercial power was lost, was that homeowners with portable generators could re-energize some down power lines when they turned on their generators in order to partially restore power to their homes.

Actual photographs of SMECO's response to the 2002 La Plata disaster were not available to me, so I had to use photographs of their response to previous disasters instead.

7-37: SMECO crew replacing utility poles.

7-38: *SMECO trucks being dispatched at night.*

This photograph shows a SMECO crew posing for a photograph after the completion of a disaster response.

7-39: *SMECO crew posing after a disaster response.*

This photograph shows Verizon employees busy installing new overhead telephone wires in La Plata. The photograph was taken by Lawrence Jackson, Jr. a staff photographer for the *Maryland Independent* newspaper.

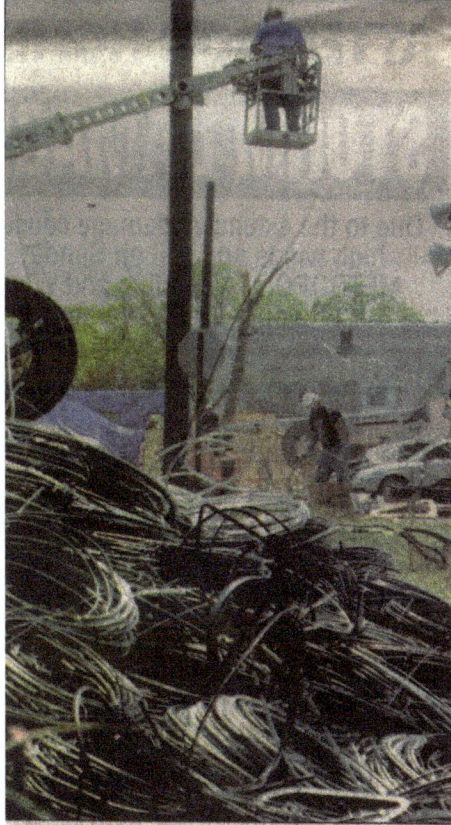

7-40: *Verizon employees installing new wires.*

In order to establish critical telecommunications in emergency conditions, Verizon brought in specialized trucks to recover satellite communication in La Plata, thus enabling mobile communications and Internet connections.

7-41: *Establishing emergency telecommunications.*

The Amish and Mennonite communities from the St. Mary's County were a 'God send for the Town' and the residents whose property was damaged or destroyed. They arrived on Monday morning and went through Town, making temporary repairs to roofs that were damaged and windows that were broken. They showed up with chainsaws and tarps to cover roofs from the weather until repairs could be made. They adamantly refused to accept any compensation and were reluctant to depend on the Town for anything. They assembled every morning in front of the 7-11 on Charles Street and spread out from there. They did accept bottles of water and even ice cream after a hard day's work. After their work was over and done with, in Charles and Calvert Counties, these communities were sent an ice cream truck on a day they were framing a new house in St. Mary's County. In addition to this treat, after it was all over the townspeople wanted to do something more long-term for their Amish and Mennonite neighbors to show them that they were really grateful for their help in time of need. These communities don't believe in insurance and none of them have health insurance. With this fact in mind, they finally agreed to accept a contribution to the fund they use to pay the medical bills when one of their people requires surgery or a hospital stay.

Because of their religious beliefs, members of these communities don't drive themselves or own cars, so volunteers from Town drove them each morning from their homes to La Plata or elsewhere wherever they would be working that day. In this photograph, the Amish are seen helping to unload a cart filled with their tools and other sundry items, which was towed behind a truck which transported them from St. Mary's County.

ANGELS IN STRAW HATS

7-42: The Amish unload their tools and supplies.

Dozens of volunteers from the Amish and Mennonite communities in St. Mary's rallied to lend a hand in the post-tornado cleanup effort. In these photographs, the Amish are seen cutting down trees and carrying branches in Quailwood.

7-43: Amish cutting down trees in Quailwood.

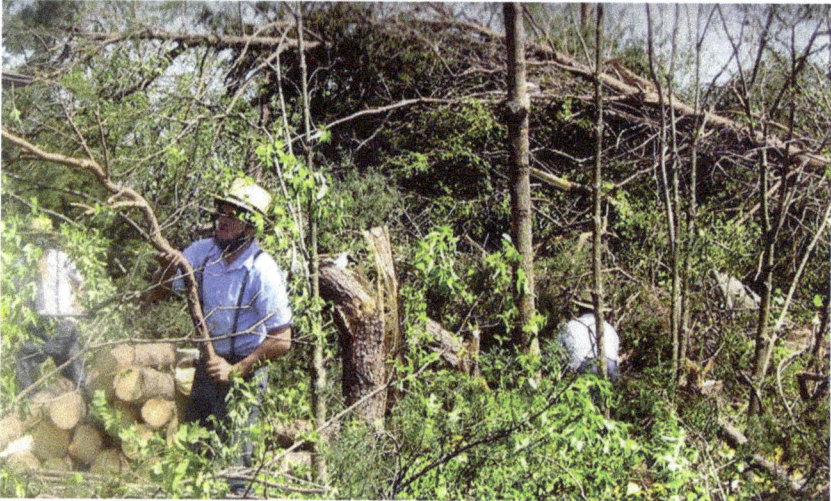

7-44: Amish hauling branches in Quailwood.

In a photograph taken by James A. Parcell of *The Washington Post*, Amish and Mennonite volunteers are seen cutting and moving branches and other debris in downtown La Plata.

7-45: Amish and Mennonite volunteers working in La Plata.

Volunteers appeared from everywhere once the tornado passed, the sky once again turned blue, and the turbulent air settled. Church groups sent scores of volunteers from Virginia, West Virginia, and all points NSEW. All were welcomed and the Town was blessed to have them come in such multitude without being asked. The following scene was shot close to the old La Plata Post Office on La Grange Avenue. The photograph appeared on the front page of the Wednesday, May 8, 2002, edition of the *Maryland Independent*. American flags flew proudly all over the town.

STAFF PHOTO BY LAWRENCE JACKSON JR.

An army of volunteers has descended on the region to help with the cleanup efforts following April 28's deadly tornado.

7-46: Volunteers were a Blessing.

PEOPLE'S PLACE

Human needs had to be met quickly and expeditiously. There were people who had lost everything to the storm. A number of buildings were totally demolished and all personal possessions, clothing, valuable papers, and all the things that a person accumulates over the years were destroyed. The initial concern was providing shelter and basic toiletry items on Sunday night, immediately after the storm went through. By Monday morning, people needed clothing and other assistance to begin to get their lives together again. The County agreed to take the lead in getting this effort organized. A number of office trailers were brought in and set up in the parking lot of the County Office Building with a large sign that said, "People's Place." Agencies such as the Red Cross, Salvation Army, Lutheran Mission Society, Catholic Charities, and others were available from the start. A number of governmental agencies were also represented, such as FEMA, the Maryland Insurance Commissioner's office, and others that were in a position to provide the assistance individuals would need. This center remained in operation for several weeks.

7-47: *The People's Place.*

BUSINESS PRESERVATION AND RESTORATION

Because La Plata is the County Seat and is located in the center of Charles County, many professionals such as doctors, dentists and lawyers, had their offices in the Downtown business district that was destroyed. The first priority was to find a place for them to re-locate. The second concern was to let their customers know where they were and how to reach them.

Some of the larger and more well-established businesses were able to bring in office trailers or temporary buildings and continue to do business in the same location or close by. The following photograph shows the office trailer CVS Pharmacy brought in within a few days and set up in the parking lot of the shopping center in front of their store in order to enable them to continue to meet the needs of their customers close to where they were originally situated before the tornado struck.

7-48: The CVS trailer.

Some business enterprises built temporary buildings, notably in those cases where their original buildings were literally destroyed. For instance, Baldus Real Estate used a temporary building as their sales office. This building was located in a vacant lot next door to the one that was destroyed by the tornado.

7-49: *The Baldus Real Estate temporary building.*

Many of the businesses that were destroyed were small businesses with very limited resources to rebuild. One of the biggest concerns was that they find temporary quarters and continue to operate in the Town rather than going out of business or relocating to Waldorf. So, the Town established a restoration center in the Town Hall to offer assistance. One of the Town Council Members was in charge of this center. Representatives of all the various organizations that might be helpful in accomplishing this goal were there and business owners were able to deal with all of the difficulties that had to be overcome in one location. Participants in this restoration center included Verizon, Southern Maryland Electric, Booz Allen IT consultants, Baldus Real Estate and the Charles County Economic Development Commission. Various state agencies, including the Department of Business and Economic Development, Maryland Department of the Environment, Maryland Department of Planning, State Insurance Commissioner, etc., were well represented at this center. FEMA also had a representative stationed there. The Executive Director of the Governor's Office of Business Advocacy and Business Assistance and his assistant helped get this Center organized. Both of them arrived in La Plata on Tuesday morning and stayed with the recovery for several months.

Verizon, operating out the restoration center in the Town Hall, had to wait for debris to be removed from the Downtown business area before new poles, serving both the needs of the telecommunication and electric power sectors, could be reestablished. In the interim, Verizon provided portable wireless phones throughout the Downtown business area.

7-50: Verizon's wireless phones.

There was some vacant office space in the Town when the tornado hit, but not all of it was in a visible or convenient location. Prominent local businessman Paul Facchina, the owner of Facchina Construction Company, was in the process of building a new building for his corporate headquarters on Centennial Street when the storm hit. La Plata Mayor Eckman related the rest of the story in his article entitled, AFTER THE STORM PASSED BY. "He came to the Town Council at a special meeting held on Monday morning and offered to build a temporary town center on land that he owned across the street from his new building. He said that he could have it ready for occupancy within a week. He warned them that to get this done he might not be able to follow all of the Town's rules and regulations. He was told that rules and regulations would not be a problem. The Town Council makes the rules and they were willing to make any changes or issue any waivers that might be needed to get the businesses back in operation. A bigger concern might be whether some of the small businesses that had lost everything because of the tornado would be able to afford the rent in addition to replacing equipment and stock they had lost. The next day he came back and said that he had solved the rent problem. When asked what the rent would be, he said that the rent would be whatever the businesses could afford. He had talked to a number of corporations that were willing to become sponsors and would subsidize the rent so that any of the businesses could afford it. He immediately began clearing the land and preparing for the temporary office buildings. A 1.7-

acre field was cleared of twisted trees, dirt was leveled, asphalt was laid, electric and sewer service was installed. All utilities were connected to the site.

BY MARK GAIL—THE WASHINGTON POST

Paul Facchina Jr., left, and Curtis Ennis place a parking barrier as they set up temporary office space in trailers Tuesday on Centennial Street in La Plata.

7-51: *Paul wasn't afraid to get his hands dirty.*

The Town had to get a special permit to move the oversize units over the Interstate Highway System, but was able to do that without causing any significant amount of delay. Within one week, on Tuesday, May 7, the temporary Town Center was complete and the first occupant, a hair dresser, opened for business. At that time, the parking lot was paved and striped, and landscaping was in place. This Center provided space for twenty businesses to operate. Some of them moved out in just a few months. Others stayed for the full two-year limit the owner had set. The following photographs show how the temporary Town Center looked when it was in full operational mode, even providing ramps for the physically challenged.

7-52: *The temporary Town Center.*

7-53: *The ramps at the temporary Town Center.*

A major component of maintaining business continuity and awareness was the task of notifying the general business community and patrons, on a timely basis, where all the displaced business entities were now temporarily relocated following the passage of the tornado. The Town did not require any type of business license, and there was no master list of what businesses and professional offices were in La Plata at the time of the tornado. One of the members of the Town Council took over the responsibility for compiling this information, and finding out where each of the displaced businesses and professional offices were now located. The Charles County Chamber of Commerce and the County Economic Development Agency were both very helpful in gathering this information. Once the information was obtained, the *Maryland Independent* newspaper included a comprehensive list of where the businesses had relocated, and how they could be reached, in the paper that was published on Friday.

Here is an example of the Charles County Maryland, "WE'RE OPEN for BUSINESS," spread that appeared in the Friday, May 10, 2002, edition of the *Maryland Independent* newspaper.

Friday, May 10, 2002 Maryland Independent

Charles County Maryland: "WE'RE OPEN for BUSINESS"

THE ONLY THING WORSE THAN LOSING OUR BUILDINGS WOULD BE TO LOSE YOUR BUSINESS.

The tornado that struck Charles County on April 28th destroyed hundreds of homes and businesses, and we are all grateful for the help that came pouring in from so many individuals, companies, and organizations. But now we are facing an even greater loss – the loss of your patronage. The publicity in the aftermath of the tornado has left the impression that our businesses are closed while we rebuild.

BUSINESS NAME	ADDRESS	CONDITION AND STATUS	PHONE
Advocacy For Family Health	406 Charles St		301-392-3877
Aline Long Skin Care Institute	P O Box 630	DESTROYED, waiting to rebuild	301-753-4181
Allstate	403 Charles St Ste 7	MOVED TO 9375 Chesapeake St., Suite # 217	301-934-4500
Alzheimers Disease Associatn	511 Charles St		301-934-5856
American Radiology Services Inc	701 Charles St		301-609-4667
American Red Cross		DESTROYED, moved to Fachinna Trailer # 103-105	301-934-2006
Annies Cleaners	6639 Old Crane Hwy	DAMAGED	301-934-1611
Archbishop Neale School	104 Port Tobacco Rd	Moved to 1st Baptist Church & Church of Latter Day Saints	301-934-9595
Baldus Real Estate Inc	P O Box 1068	DESTROYED, moved TO 5 Maple Ave.	301-934-8407
Barbour Zverina Buchanan	P O Box 1098		301-934-2241
Beltone Hearing Aid Center	115a La Grange Ave	DAMAGED, will rebuild	301-609-9615
Benjamin L Jenkins Jr MD	P O Box 1724	DESTROYED MOVED TO LaPlata Prof Bldg by 7-11	301-934-2887
Blessed Lambs Pre-School	3 Port Tobacco Rd	DESTROYED, closed for the year, will rebuild	301-934-2269
Burger King	6720 Crain Hwy	DESTROYED, but will rebuild	301-609-7455
Buyers Title Inc	201 Centennial St	DAMAGED MOVED TO 9375 Chesapeake St. Suite #209	301-753-1000
Casey Jones Restaurant	P O Box 1587	DAMAGED, will reopen in 1 week	301-932-6226
Chapman Bowling Scott & Hrud	P O Box 610	MOVED TO 9375 Chesapeake St Suite # 200-225	301-870-5355
Chapel Point Development Corp	107 Howard Street	MOVED TO 9375 Chesapeake Street, Suite 223	301-870-4430
Charles County Rescue Squad	2 Calvert Street	DAMAGED, moved to Old Fire House	
Choice Professional Resources	401 Carroll St	DAMAGED, moved to Fachinna Trailer # 137	
Cleaning Concepts	401 Charles St	DAMAGED - Temporarily Closed	301-609-9045

7-54: *We're open for your business.*

FINANCING THE RECOVERY

The Town received a lot of financial help from a number of different sources. Within the first few days, the County provided $150,000 and the State donated $100,000 to take care of the immediate expenses. Neither of these grants were designated for any particular purpose, and they were used to cover the initial costs associated with the cleanup of the Town. One way the funds were used was to pay bills for lodging, meals, fuel, and other expenses for the volunteer help that came from all over the state and elsewhere. The biggest contributions came from the State of

Maryland. The Governor committed a total of $1,400,000 immediately to help the Town rebuild according to its Vision Plan. We'll talk much more about this Plan and the monies from government, state, individuals, and other sources used for rebuilding La Plata within the blueprint of this Plan in the next chapter.

Before we leave the subject of recovery following the passage of the tornado, allow me to present some comments concerning FEMA's role in all of this from different perspectives.

Mayor Eckman expressed his view of FEMA's role in his article.

> *"On Wednesday morning, representatives from FEMA arrived and announced that they were there to take care of the cleanup. They said that the insurance companies were responsible for cleaning up the buildings they had insured. They also said that each property owner would have to separate wooden waste and hazardous materials from the remains of the buildings before it was hauled away. The Mayor and the President of the County Commissioners objected strongly to that approach. For one thing, the question would arise as to which insurance company was responsible for what. The remains of some buildings were scattered over a four-block area. Would each property owner be responsible for going over the entire area, collecting the remains of their buildings, and hauling them away? Or would individual insurance companies be responsible for getting rid of debris from other property owner's buildings that ended up on the property they had insured? And even if these questions could be resolved, cleaning up property by property would take all summer. The resources to do the job were available right then. The cleanup had already been scheduled to begin within the next week. Both the Mayor and the County Commission President were adamant that they intended to proceed as planned and to stay on schedule."*

In another section of his article, the Mayor made this comment"

"There was some thought that FEMA would reim-burse them for their actual expenses. While FEMA would have paid for hiring workers and equipment, they refused to pay anything toward the help the Town received on a volunteer basis. They based their refusal on the fact that the Town did not have a formal mutual aid agreement with any of these entities and FEMA said that they weren't required to come to the aid of La Plata. Since they were not required to do it, FEMA considered it a volunteer action and they don't pay volunteers."

In addition, Tom and Jane O'Farrell, who once lived at 104 Oak Avenue in La Plata, told me that someone from FEMA came to their damaged house and only offered "emotional support" to them instead of offering something they really needed: help removing the debris from around their house.

On a positive note, FEMA did publish a flyer entitled, *Recovery Times*, which provided valuable information regarding various sources of aid available to victims, including SBA (Small Business Administration (SBA) low interest loans. The flyer also had recovery information, such as how to file an insurance claim, disaster assistance questions and answers, and other pertinent recovery information.

MARYLAND TORNADO

Recovery Times

Published by the Federal Emergency Management Agency and the Maryland Emergency Management Agency

MARYLAND/ May 10, 2002/ FEMA Vol. 1

The flag flies over this home, one of many damaged or destroyed by the April 28 tornado

FEMA photo by Liz Roll

IMPORTANT RECOVERY INFORMATION

■Register by Phone
Residents of declared counties whose homes, businesses or personal property sustained damage as a result of April 28 tornado are urged to begin the application process. Call **800-621-FEMA (3362)** from 8 a.m. to 6 p.m. seven days a week. Those with speech or hearing impairments should call 800-462-7585.

■Disaster Housing Assistance
The Federal Emergency Management Agency (FEMA) may pay for temporary rental housing, hotel/motel expenses, mortgage or rental payments to prevent foreclosure or eviction resulting from the storms or essential repairs to make the home habitable.

■U.S. Small Business Administration
During disasters, the U.S. Small Business Administration (SBA) provides low-interest, long-term loans to homeowners, renters and businesses of all sizes that are not fully insured.

■Safe Rooms
Safe rooms can provide protection from winds up to 250 miles an hour. For details, order *"Taking Shelter from the Storm"* from FEMA publications (800-480-2520) or visit the FEMA at www.fema.gov/mit/saferoom/.

**Apply by Phone
800-621-FEMA**
TTY: 800-462-7585
8 a.m. to 6 p.m.
seven days a week

Disaster aid available now

Three southern Maryland counties were ripped by a fierce tornado on April 28 leaving a swath of devastation in its wake. Governor Parris Glendening called upon President Bush to provide help from the federal government in cleaning up and repairing the damage.

FEMA Director Joe M. Allbaugh announced that, in response to that request, President Bush directed on May 1 that a federal disaster be declared to provide help to individuals and businesses in the affected areas who suffered disaster-related damage.

The disaster-designated counties are Calvert, Charles and Dorchester. Allbaugh indicated damage assessments are continuing and more counties and assistance may be designated later based on the results of these surveys.

The disaster declaration enables FEMA and other federal agencies to team up with state and local disaster workers to help residents and business owners in the affected counties recover from the storms.

Government disaster assistance covers basic needs, but will not normally compensate disaster victims for their entire loss. If you have insurance, the government may help pay for basic needs not covered under your insurance policy. The types of help available are outlined in this newsletter and will be explained when you call to register for aid.

Those affected by the storms who live or own businesses in one of the disaster-declared areas may apply for aid by calling: **800-621-FEMA (800-621-3362)**. Speech- and hearing-impaired persons should call 800-462-7585.

7-55: An Issue of the Recovery Times.

CHAPTER 8
A New Beginning

After residential homeowners received monies to rebuild from their insurance companies, or received loans from the Small Business Administration, it was sincerely hoped that most of these residents took heed of suggestions of the National Weather Service damage assessment survey team recommendations when rebuilding their new homes. These suggestions are in alignment with the existing building code for Southern Maryland, at that time, being the International Residential Code for One and Two-Family Dwellings published by the International Code Council (2000). The suggestions were based on observations of how well variously designed and constructed homes fared when faced with the extreme wind forces of the tornado. This pertained mainly to homes which lost their roofs, or slid off their foundations, or both as a result of the passage of the tornado.

Roofing: Adding a few extra nails to roof coverings made a significant difference for homes on the periphery of the vortex. Also, tie-down straps did help hold down roof assemblies.

Foundations: Install foundation anchors or straps.

Remember those two homes damaged on Hill Spring Drive?

8-1: *The two Hill Spring Drive homes: Before.*

Those homes have been beautifully rebuilt and are hardly recognizable from the 2002 damage photograph. Google Maps provided this image.

8-2: *The two Hill Spring Drive homes: After.*

These are some before and after photographs of residential homes in the Quailwood Subdivision.

8-3: *Residential homes in Quailwood: Before.*

Here is the same location as seen on Google Maps.

8-4: *Residential homes in Quailwood: After.*

Remember those residential homes at the end of Hawkins Gate Road which were affected by what appeared to be two vortexes within the same tornado? The original photograph taken by Tim Marshall, which I adapted, is shown once again as a frame of reference.

8-5: Homes at the end of Hawkins Gate Road: Before.

The adapted image obtained from Google Maps shows these residential homes today.

8-6: Homes at the end of Hawkins Gate Road: After.

These homes at the end of Normandie Woods Drive and East Patuxent Drive and Route 6 (Charles Street), which were once demolished by the tornado, have been rebuilt as seen in a Google Maps view adjusted by the author to match the same vantage damage perspective.

8-7: Homes at Normandie Woods Drive and East Patuxent Drive: Before.

**8-8: *Homes at Normandie Woods Drive
and East Patuxent Drive: After.***

Within the Town of La Plata itself, the forward-looking Mayor the Town Council had already planned for the revitalization of the Downtown area long before the tornado struck. In addition, a number of business proprietors, like Mary Martin, had been thinking for years about renovating their establishments and modernizing their businesses.

PLANNING FOR THE FUTURE

In 1999, three years before the tornado, the Town hired a team of consultants to explore the vision the residents had for the future of the Town and prepare a plan to accomplish it. The plan focused on creating a new Town Center north of Charles Street. The primary purpose of this Town Center would be to serve as a catalyst to create a better sense of community among residents of the Town. Most of the single-family residences that have been built in recent years were in clearly defined subdivisions. New residents, business people, and property owners of La Plata and the surrounding area came together five times for full day planning workshops. As a result of these meetings, the consultants prepared a "Vision Plan for Greater La Plata" that the Mayor and Council adopted in March of 2000. A Vision implementation team was appointed and met regularly to develop an action plan to accomplish the vision. As a result of their efforts, the Mayor and Council adopted an Urban Design for Downtown La Plata in March of 2001. As depicted below:

8-9: The Urban Design Plan for Downtown La Plata.

The plan was to eventually demolish nearly everything north of Charles Street and build a new Town Center. The implementation team continued to meet, and by April of 2002, the team had nearly completed a series of design guidelines for commercial properties, and laid the groundwork for a Design Review Board to administer them.

There were four basic goals included in the Urban Design Plan that would be incorporated into the plan to rebuild the Town.

1. Create a walking Downtown that would become a destination for the remainder of Charles County and Southern Maryland.

2. Increase the density in the Downtown.

3. Encourage mixed use buildings with businesses on the first floor and residences on the upper floors to increase the number of people within walking distance of the Central Business District.

4. Attract more retail and service businesses to the Downtown.

As a result of all this preliminary work, the Mayor and Council knew what they wanted to accomplish and had the basis for a plan to rebuild the Town.

THE FUTURE IS NOW

But as we already know, Mother Nature had her own plan for redesigning Downtown La Plata. She executed her plan during the evening hours of April 28, 2002, in no uncertain terms.

8-10: *The path of the tornado through La Plata.*

The tornado virtually destroyed the entire Central Business District, technically wiping the slate clean for most of the businesses and their properties which were in existence on the morning of Sunday, April 28, 2002.

The tornado thus provided the impetus for the Town to immediately implement its Plan when it suddenly struck like a sudden bolt from the sky. However, such an ambitious Vision Plan cost lots of money, and who but the State of Maryland and its distinguished Governor came through for the Town? Much of the success of the recovery effort was due to their in-depth knowledge of State Government, and their willingness to be there when they were needed.

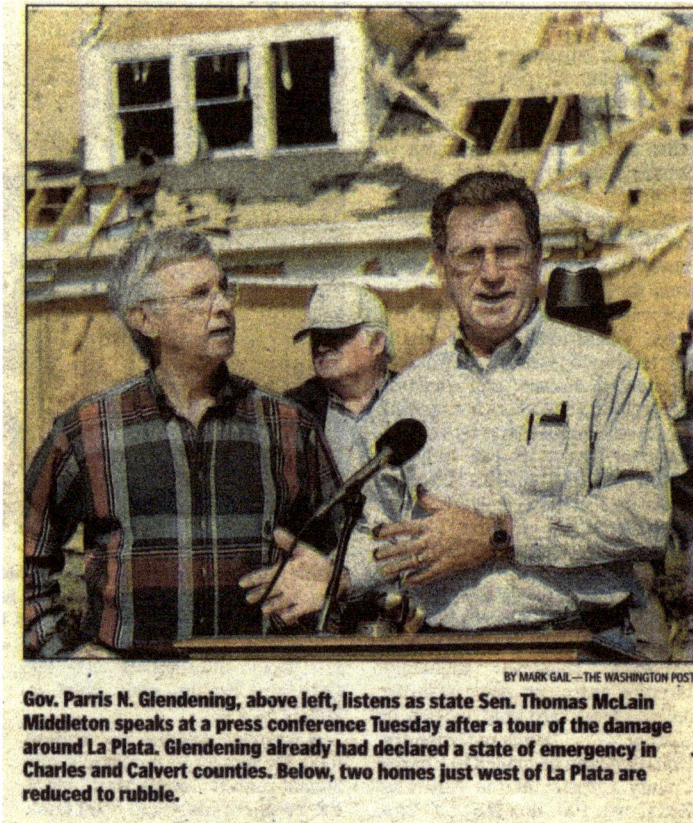

BY MARK GAIL—THE WASHINGTON POST

Gov. Parris N. Glendening, above left, listens as state Sen. Thomas McLain Middleton speaks at a press conference Tuesday after a tour of the damage around La Plata. Glendening already had declared a state of emergency in Charles and Calvert counties. Below, two homes just west of La Plata are reduced to rubble.

8-11: A Proactive Governor.

When Governor Glendenning and his staff arrived the Tuesday morning after the tornado struck, he was "ready to kick ass and take names." He announced that the State was going to contribute over $2 million dollars to help the Town rebuild. He said that a check for $100,000 would arrive within the week, and that the Town could use it however it saw fit to take care of its immediate needs. That check arrived within the week, and it was one of the few times that the Town ever received anything from the State with no strings attached. Then there would be $1.4 million dollars available to enable La Plata to build back according to its Vision Plan. The Governor also promised that the Town would receive all kinds of assistance from state agencies.

GOING MY WAY

In his article "After the Storm Passed," the Mayor talked about the initial apprehension amongst property owners, both business and homeowners, about the Town's Vision Plan and the incentives (carrots) the Town offered to these property owners if they followed the Town's lead: "Talks about the Town's Vision Plan generated a lot of concern within the Town and rumors were rampant." Many of the business and property owners were afraid that the Town would not allow them to rebuild what they had before the tornado went through. Some thought they wouldn't be able to afford the type of buildings the Urban Design Plan recommended. A meeting was held at Casey Jones Restaurant and Pub in the center of the damaged area on that first Thursday evening. The Mayor assured the business owners that the Town would allow them to build back just what they had before if that is what they wanted to do. If the zoning and other regulations had changed since their building was originally built, the Town would waive various provisions or even change the Town Code if that was what it took to allow them to rebuild. The only two conditions that weren't negotiable were that the plans had to be signed by a registered architect, and that the building would have to meet all the current building code requirements. The Mayor also told them that if they decided to rebuild according to the Town's Vision Plan, they would get a lot of help.

1. The Town would assist the property owners in dealing with their insurance company if the adjusters objected to changing the footprint of the building or its location on the lot.

2. Storm water management regulations would be relaxed or waived.

3. Parking requirements would be relaxed, changed, or actually waived in some situations.

4. The Town would assist the property owners to qualify for low interest loans.

5. Building permits and other fees would be waived.

6. Property owners would receive tax credits from both the Town and the County to counteract the increased value of the new buildings.

7. They would receive special incentive grants to cover the cost of a new foundation or relocating their buildings.

In return for all of these incentives, the property owners would be expected to work with the Town in developing a plan to rebuild in a way that was in accordance with the Town's Vision Plan. While there were some concerns expressed, the tone of the initial meeting was very positive. Everyone seemed willing to rebuild in a way that would make La Plata a better place to live, work, and do business than it was before the tornado. A Design Review Board (DRB) was established and given the responsibility of reviewing all plans for new buildings within the storm damaged area, and making recommendations to the Town Council as to the amount of incentive grant each of them should receive. The DRB included an architect, two businessmen, and two residents of the Town. As work progressed on implementing the Vision Plan, it became obvious that there were some conflicts between the design guidelines and the zoning regulations of the Town.

As an example, a bank and some real estate offices had been destroyed on the corner of Charles Street and Route 301. The owner proposed to replace three buildings with a very imposing building that would be several times larger than the total square footage it replaced. This building would be located at the entrance to the Town's business district and was just what the Vision Plan recommended. The initial design included a drive-in window at the same place the old bank had it, facing Charles Street. The DRB objected to the location because the view of the building would be obscured by cars waiting in line to get to the drive-in window instead of a nicely landscaped area. The problem was the fact that this building would be located in a highway commercial zone and the required setback was forty-five feet from the property line. The property line at that location was actually more than twelve feet from the curb and following the regulations meant that the building would actually be sixty feet from the road. Since that intersection was the entranceway to the Town's business district, a new urban highway zone was created for that general area that allowed a setback of only fifteen feet if the building met certain standards. As a result of this change, the drive-in window was moved to the other side of the building with access from the parking lot. A very nicely landscaped entrance now faces Charles Street instead of a line of cars waiting to go through the drive-in lane. The following photographs show the first impression a person has of the Town when they enter La Plata from Route 301, traveling either northbound or southbound.

8-12: Entering the Town of La Plata from the north on US 301.

8-13: Entering the Town of La Plata from the south on US 301.

The State of Maryland, under Governor Glendenning, created a Neighborhood Conservation program that was intended to improve the streetscape when a state highway went through a municipality. This included such things as building new sidewalks, new streetlights, and adding landscaping to mark the difference between a rural highway and the main street of a Town. One of the main goals of La Plata's Vision Plan was to qualify for a Neighborhood Conservation Program to make Charles Street the main street of La Plata rather than just another section of State Route 6. This Highway was one of the major links between Route 301 and Route 5, the primary highway entering St. Mary's County, and much of the congestion in Downtown La Plata was caused by through traffic. These programs had always been limited to state highways. In the case of La Plata, the Governor agreed to extend the program to cover the entire area damaged by the tornado. In the end, most of the improvements that were made were on town streets, not state highways. The Town's Vision Plan included extending Centennial Street from La Grange Avenue to South Maple Avenue. The Streetscape Project as it was approved was planned to be built in four phases. The initial phase was to rebuild the heart of the damaged area focusing on La Grange Avenue, Centennial Street, and Maple Avenue. The second phase would cover Charles Street. The next phase would improve St. Mary's Avenue, and the final phase would rebuild Oak Avenue and other streets that were not as severely damaged. The work as planned was completed in six months.

STREETSCAPE PROJECT

8-14: *The Streetscape Project.*

This Google Map shows a modern view of the results of the Town's Vision Plan.

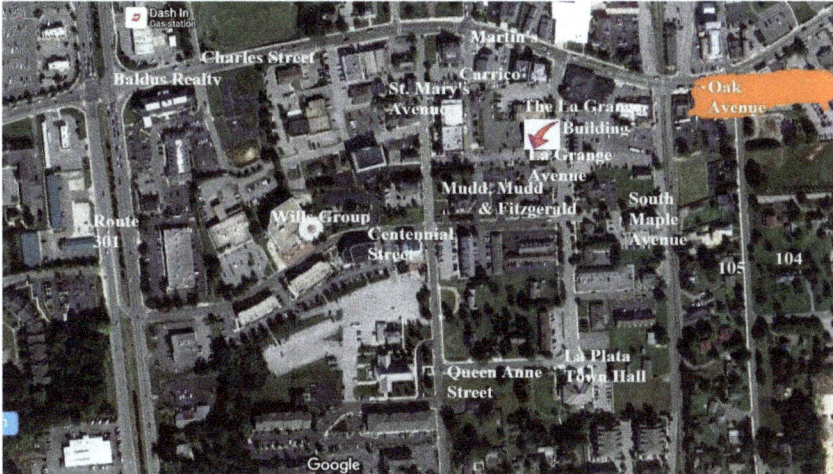

8-15: *Modern view of STREETSCAPE Project.*

Different approaches to rebuilding were taken by businesses and homeowners depending on their own individual feasibility, situation and practicality.

The Carrico Building, located at 303 Charles Street, was heavily damaged by the tornado, but remained basically intact. The La Plata **Memory Lane Exhibit** related the following:

The 7 children of Rudolf and Thomas Carrico were committed to preserving the historical character of the structure, and also creating an aesthetically pleasing modernized building in the middle of La Plata. The building expanded on the 1st and 2nd floors by creating new space within the original footprint. The entry foyer has been enhanced with tile flooring and an elevator, which complements the old staircase and the front door that survived the tornado. The furnace and radiators have been replaced by individual HVAC units for each apartment and office. Hardwood flooring was installed in the upstairs apartments and hallways. The kitchens and bathrooms boast modern appliances, fixtures and tile. The building has new windows, insulation and sprinklers. The new exterior siding and lighting were designed to preserve the character of the building while also providing a "facelift".

8-16: *The Carrico building approach to revitalization.*

8-17: The Carrico building: Before and After.

Martin's is located at 309 Charles Street. It was totally destroyed by the tornado and had to be rebuilt from the ground up, according to Marty Martin. It took fourteen months to rebuild. During this time, Marty, his wife Caroline, and his family visited such historical sites as Jamestown and Williamsburg, Virginia in order to get inspiration for designing their new establishment. "We had considered rebuilding before the storm, but it was not feasible for us. Our old building did not meet some of the new codes, and was not handicapped accessible in some areas. Once we got over the initial shock and got through the insurance process, it was exciting to plan and construct a new, more modern, and larger building. We were able to double our size and add a gift shop in the front." Immediately after the tornado, Marty had to service cars in his home shop, but now he has six service bays, fully equipped with the latest diagnostic and testing equipment in order to serve his loyal customers.

8-18: *Martin's Before and After.*

The La Grange Building, located at 109 La Grange Avenue, was virtually destroyed by the passing of the tornado.

8-19: *The La Grange Building after the tornado struck.*

However, the **Memory Lane Exhibit** relates a much happier ending for this building.

Fortunately with the encouragement of the Town of La Plata the building was back bigger and better. With the guidance and encouragement from the town what was a tragic devastation turned into a great opportunity to build back better than ever. Previously it was a masonry block building, today it is a brick and masonry building, with a modern sprinkler system, wired for internet and modern communications and offering 3 larger apartments than the original building. The building was bought by Marty and Caroline Martin in 2004 and they continue to operate it today.

8-20: *The story has a happy ending.*

8-21: *The La Grange Building today*

The long and proud tradition and heritage of the Sydney E. Mudd House at 106 St. Mary's was beautifully captured in the **Memory Lane Exhibit**.

8-22: *The renovation of the Mudd House.*

The wind of the La Plata tornado of April 28, 2002, scattered the second level of the Mudd, Mudd, & Fitzgerald Law Office in all directions, swept through the first floor, relocating throughout the Town of La Plata anything not nailed down. Virtually all furnishings were scarred, otherwise damaged, or rendered worthless. Bookkeeping and other legal records maintained on the second floor were found as far away as Seaford, Delaware, and gratefully returned by astonished residents on the Eastern Shore of the Chesapeake Bay.

The building housing the law office was constructed in 1894 by U.S. Senator Sydney E. Mudd. Following the passage of the tornado, considerable thought was given to preserving the original premises following the guidelines of the Mayor's Vision Plan. Mudd, Mudd, & Fitzgerald was back in business in early May of 2002 serving its clients from temporary facilities located on the north side of Charles Street opposite the Civista Hospital.

The response to the virtual demolition of the building by the attorneys in residence and their immediate families was overwhelming, even passersby with no association with the attorneys or their staff stopped in sifting through the debris, to lend a hand to pull furniture from the rubble, etc. True to tradition, the Amish community was there to assist in any way they could.

Although unable to preserve the original 1894 structure, a new office exteriorly replicating the 1894 structure was formally reopened for business in July 2003. Original siding, window trim, door hardware, mantels, and foundation brick, salvaged from the debris, were incorporated into the new facility. Several interior spaces were meticulously copied to the original areas.

In October 2020, the property at 106 St. Mary's Avenue become the new home of the Dream Big (DB) Boutique and Business Center. The firm of Mudd, Mudd & Fitzgerald moved to 116 La Grange Avenue. According to their sign in front, the boutique offers jewelry, gifts, home décor, and more. The sign still says "Sydney E. Mudd House."

8-23: *The Dream Big Boutique.*

Oak Avenue in La Plata is noted for its historic Victorian-style homes, and of course its trademark stance of tall, sturdy oak trees lining the street. On April 28, 2002, fierce winds tore down many of the picturesque trees, and ravaged many of the beautiful homes. Many were ripped opened like a can of sardines, their contents scattered to the four winds. The restoration of the home belonging to Tom and Jane O'Farrell at 104 Oak Avenue was featured in an article entitled, *Almost Gone with the Wind*, which appeared in the magazine, **This Old House** of May 2005. The O'Farrells shared their story with my son, and I when we visited them at their home in Hagerstown, they were determined to adhere as close as they could to the Town's Vision Plan in the restoration of their home, trying desperately to maintain the historic character of the house without going into debt. Read their entire story in the **This Old House** article. It is an interesting and fascinating story of their trials and tribulations in trying to save their old house without going into debt themselves.

Let's first take a look at what the O'Farrells found when they returned home on April 29, 2002.

8-24: The O'Farrell home after the tornado struck.

After two years of hard work, much of it done by Tom and Jane themselves, a little help from friends and volunteers, and a lot of luck, imagination, and ingenuity, their home was restored. Here is a photograph of their renovated, old house.

*8-25: **The O'Farrell home after renovation.***

Another of these beautiful, Victorian-style homes which was restored, was located at 105 Oak Avenue. Here is what the home looked like after the passage of the tornado.

*8-26: **105 Oak Avenue after the tornado struck.***

The owners maintained the basic footprint of its original design as much as possible.

8-27: 105 Oak Avenue renovated.

With the interest in extending Centennial Street to South Maple Street, under the Vision Plan, came the construction of beautifully designed office buildings. One such building was the one built by the Wills Group in 2002 at 102 Centennial Street.

8-28: The Wills Group Building.

The showcase for me of the La Plata "Vision Plan" is the Town Hall, located at 305 Queen Ann Street. It was completed in 2004. It architecturally possesses the aesthetics balance between the need for a traditional exterior and integration with surrounding civic green space with a requirement for modern interior conveniences. The structure was the first LEED-certified building in Charles County, Maryland. The new Town Hall was built in the center of Town, as the Vision Plan recommended, to bring more focus on the area that was rebuilt after the tornado.

8-29: *The La Plata Town Hall.*

The La Plata Town Hall houses various departments, including public works, operations, inspections, planning, and zoning. It also includes the offices of the town mayor, manager, treasurer, and clerk. The town hall maintains several boards, committees and commissions that address various matters throughout the town, including beautification, design review, and appeals. La Plata Town Hall also has a parks and recreation department that operates several parks and administers a range of recreational activities and programs.

8-30: *The interior of the Town Hall.*

In its design of the Town Hall, KGD Architecture strove to achieve an aesthetics balance between the need for a traditional exterior and integration with surrounding civic green space with a requirement for modern interior conveniences.

8-31: *Modern interior layout.*

You may recall that the Jameson Manor Farm, located at 7061Olivers Shop Road near Hughesville, suffered major damage due the passage of the tornado.

8-32: The Jameson Manor Farm: Before.

Following the tornado, a number of changes were made to the farm, including the placement of the main house and the addition of a number of new structures, including barns and other utility buildings.

8-33: The Jameson Manor Farm: After.

CHAPTER 9
Lessons Learned

Mayor William F. Eckman
(Mayor of the Town of La Plata, 1983-2005)

You've Got to Have a Plan. The Town hadn't done much preparation for tornadoes. Even though a killer tornado had struck La Plata in 1926, basically no disaster plans were in place prior to April 28, 2002.

Maintain personal relationships with other agencies and levels of government in order to ensure prompt and timely response to emergencies when needed.

Establish a clear delineation of responsibilities between the Town and County for each facet of the recovery phase of an emergency.

Ensure the presence of high-level, onsite government officials possessing the power to make decisions and see that these decisions are fully implemented once they are made.

People will be there when they are needed if they are aware of what's happening.

Bill Murray
(Meteorologist, President of the Weather Factory)

"The lessons learned are not new: established office policies must be followed to facilitate communication of critical information and ensure proper storm monitoring. **Supercells often display cycles of weakening and intensification. Forecasters should always be slow to downgrade from a tornado warning.** The severe thunderstorm warning issued at 6:45 p.m. did carry the familiar line, "Severe thunderstorms can produce tornadoes with little or no advance warning." This is important advice for all of us whenever severe thunderstorm warnings are issued. When it comes to thunderstorms, expect the unexpected!"

Need for National Weather Service warning forecaster to be notified of any previous tornado landfalls. This was not the case in the La Plata tornado when only a severe thunderstorm warning was made at 6:45 p.m., rather than an actual tornado warning. **NOTE: A category F2 tornado had previously made touchdown in the Shenandoah Valley at 4:55 p.m., but this fact was never reported to these forecasters.**

Excerpt from the NWS *Service Assessment*, La Plata, Maryland, Tornado Outbreak,

> *April 28, 2002.*
> *Warning and Forecast Services - WFO Baltimore/ Washington*
> *During the Event.*
> *FACT: Without a confirmed tornado report, and believing the supercell's tornadic potential was decreasing, the warning forecasters issued a severe thunderstorm warning for Charles and Calvert Counties at 6:45 p.m.*
> *FACT: At 7:02 p.m., six minutes after the tornado touched down (in Marbury), a tornado warning was issued for Charles and Calvert Counties.*

However, it was noted that the Baltimore/Washington Weather Forecasting Office (WFO) breached the NWS Eastern Region Headquarters Severe Weather Best Practices guidelines by not following the "prior offender" rule: "Once an offender, keep following until it is completely dissipated and no longer a threat." While radar had indicated weakening of the bow echo signature at the surface, there was still a mesocyclone at the upper levels of the atmosphere. Further, "When supercells are possible and/or indicated by radar, it is important to err on the side of safety and issue a tornado warning," and "Since supercells are relatively rare, we are not increasing the FAR (False Alarm Rate) much if a given supercell... doesn't produce a tornado."

NWS Service Assessment

The Charles County Emergency Management Director stated he needs more advance notice and would like a "heads up" when severe weather is over Virginia, and before warnings are issued for southern Maryland. Topper Shutt, Chief Meteorologist at the TV station WUSA Channel 9 in Washington, D.C., said, "[WFO] Sterling could have been a little ahead of the game with the Charles County tornado warning..."

Only the National Weather Service can determine the rating of a tornado based on the results of an actual on-site survey done by its damage experts, which included Tim Marshall of Haag Engineering. The public was erroneously notified that the La Plata tornado was rated as an F5 when the follow-up National Weather Service damage experts determined that it was actually an F4. Meteorologists criticized the 1996 blockbuster film *Twister* because the actors kept announcing Fujita (F) ratings of tornadoes they were tracking before an actual National Weather Service damage survey team had made any kind of assessment.

The public dissemination of pertinent tornado weather information in Charles County, as well as in La Plata, was inadequate and lacking. An April 29, 2002, a *Washington Post* article stated, "despite tornado alerts that the NWS began issuing, many people said they had known nothing about the impending danger." An April 29, 2002, *The New York Times* article quoted Charles County spokeswoman, Nina W. Voehl, "the National Weather Service issued a tornado warning **(watch) [sic]** four hours before La Plata was hit. But residents said they became aware of one only when they saw the tornado and heard it." This was confirmed in interviews where most people said they were not paying close attention to the media on a Sunday afternoon.

Timothy P. Marshall
(Haag Engineering Company)

THE LA PLATA, MD TORNADO: ISSUES REGARDING THE F-SCALE. Residential homes built in La Plata must be built in accordance with the existing building code for Southern Maryland: the International Residential Code for One and Two-Family Dwellings published by the International Code Council (2000). This code requires that sill plates be secured to the foundation with anchor bolts spaced a maximum of six feet apart. Also, anchor bolts must be located within twelve inches of the ends of each plate section. Foundation anchor straps are acceptable as long as they provide the same strength as 1.27-cm (1/2-inch) bolts. Therefore, homes not anchored or strapped to their foundations did not conform to provisions in the building code. Interestingly, the code also indicates that foundation walls must have vertical steel reinforcement to provide a continuous load path for both gravity (dead) loads and wind uplift. We found that none of the homes that slid off their foundations due to the passage of the tornado met this requirement.

"Houses that slid off their foundations were not attached adequately and failed at relatively low wind speeds. In some instances, failures were the result of building code violations. However, in other instances, there were contradictions in the building code," said Marshall. "It is the author's opinion that straight- and toe-nailing of wooden connections must be augmented by straps or clips to provide better pull-out resistance necessary to meet or exceed the wind uplift requirements in the building codes."

Kathryn Newman

Kathryn helped her patent attorney husband, David, operate a law firm at 201 Centennial Street in La Plata. Their office was located on the top third floor of the building. The wind lifted the roof off of its moorings, shifting it, and bursting the water pipes. It shattered some windows and blew out others, frame and all completely out of the wall. It literally gutted the entire inside structure.

In an article entitled, **Rehoboth homeowners survive destructive La Plata Tornado,** as written by Billy E. Taylor, Jr. for *The Coast Press*, she offered her advice to small business owners, especially to other law firms. "Her message is clear. You must be prepared to save yourself and then be ready to recoup your business losses."

Some of Newman's most important points to having your business prepared are:

Know your insurance policies. Know what losses are covered.

Get business interruption insurance. This kind of coverage will pay a percentage of your income stream as you rebuild your client files and case information.

Have a master list of client information stored off-site in a safe place, such as a safety deposit box. Insurance policies and copies of other critical papers should be also be kept there.

Do a comprehensive asset inventory and keep that in a safe place.

Back up computer files and servers and keep them off-site.

CHAPTER 10
Preparing for the Future

"Those who fail to learn from history are doomed to repeat it."
—*Sir Winston Churchill*

Nearly fourteen years to the day after the April 28, 2002, F4 tornado struck La Plata, a very threatening monster supercell crossed the Potomac River not far from Marbury, Maryland, then moved southeast near Ripley and approached La Plata around 7:00 p.m. EDT. **Sound familiar?** The date was May 2, 2016.

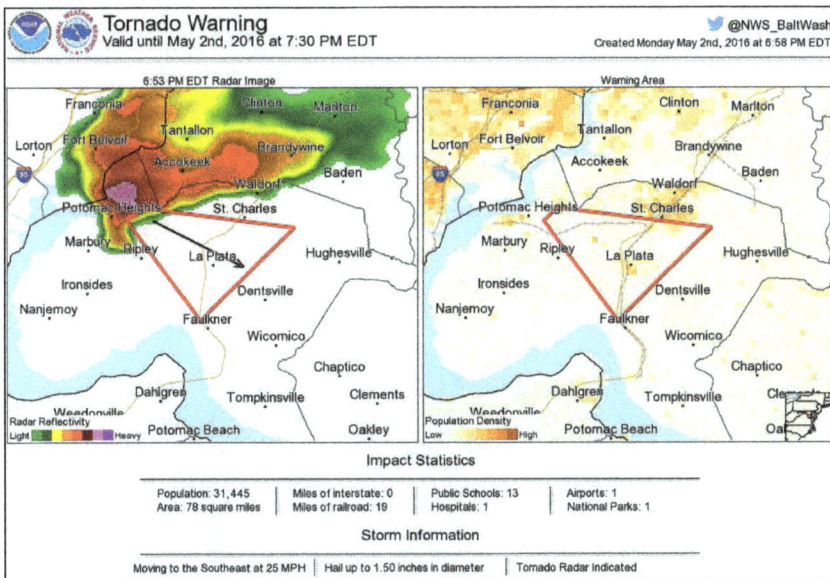

10-1: *Tornado warning, National Weather Service.*
Baltimore/Washington, May 2, 2016.

Fortunately for La Plata, the supercell was just a show of force and caused no damage, but probably resulted in some heart flutters among the populace.

10-2: Another La Plata supercell storm?

Charles County is certainly no stranger to tornadic and other severe weather and non-weather emergency events. In fact, from 1950 to 2000, thirteen tornadoes struck the county according to Barbara Watson with the National Weather Service.

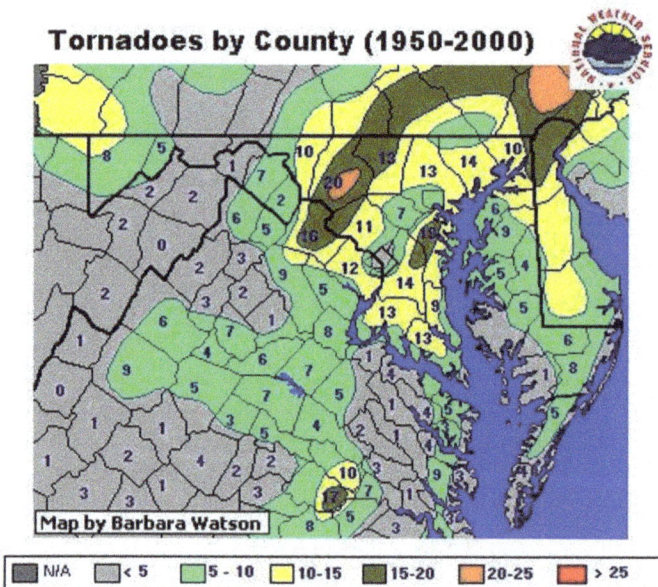

10-3: Tornadoes by Maryland County, 1950 to 2000.

At the time of the April 28, 2002 tornado, how prepared was Charles County's emergency response structure for the disaster which was to come? I think George Gershwin's classic song, "I Got Plenty o' Nuttin," probably best describes the status of this preparedness. According to Tony Rose, the Deputy Director of Charles County Emergency Services, there was no Emergency Operations Center, no large-scale-wide area incident management plan or mechanism in place, few computers in place, no efficient way of communicating with 9-1-1 operation centers in nearby Virginia about weather related events (remember the tornado traveled through Virginia and made landfall in western Charles County), and a scarcity of vehicles. There were just three equipped with emergency communications and stand-alone emergency supplies and equipment. Tony explains in more detail, "We were caught in the midst of a technology / sophistication transition. As fate would have it, the new 9-1-1 Center, including a new Emergency Operations Center and our new public safety radio system, were all under construction when the tornado struck. As a matter of fact, we had only recently taken delivery of our mobile command and communication bus. This vehicle is equipped with radio and telephone equipment to support large scale incident management. We used it extensively during our response to this tornado."

Tony concludes by saying, "At the time of the tornado, the Department of Emergency Services was a relatively new and evolving department within the Charles County Government. On the other hand, volunteer Fire and EMS were firmly established and did in fact respond in force and provided the critical services you would expect. Montgomery County sent us their incident management team for support, and Ocean City sent us their Emergency Manager. The lunch room at the Charles County government building was converted to our Emergency Operations Center. The Commissioners' hearing room was used as a briefing room where Department of Emergency Services (DES), volunteer Fire / EMS, law enforcement and a host of response partners collaborated to recover from this assault. At the time of this event, the County had the Charles County Emergency Operations Plan (EOP) that included several annexes, including a plan to address response to a tornado. We were familiar with response to F0 and F1 tornados, but not with the devastating effects of a monstrous F4 tornado."

There was a problem letting people know that the tornado was coming and that they needed to take shelter before it hit. Most public places in La Plata now have First Alert Weather Alert Radios in order to provide early warning NOAA tornado alerts, watches, and warnings.

10-4: *First Alert Weather Alert Radio.*

In addition, the various county governments in southern Maryland have made arrangements with Public Access Television Stations (PATS) in the area to transmit a warning to all television sets that are turned on when the National Weather Service issues a tornado watch or warning.

Public Access Television Stations	
Channel 95 or FIOS 10	Charles County Government
Comcast Cable Channel 6	Calvert County Government
Channel 95	St. Mary's County Government

10-5: PATS.

Finally, the Charles County Citizen Notification System (CNS) – Powered by EverBridge, is a free service that allows anyone to receive emergency, weather, and community notifications via phone calls, text messages, and e-mail for any location in Charles County. The CNS provides updates and alerts from the Charles County Government and the National Weather Service.

10-6: **The CNS.**

The Charles County Government's Department of Emergency Services (DES) is the focal point for emergency preparedness and response activities for the county. The facility is physically located at 10425 Audie Lane in La Plata, just off Radio Station Road. This facility houses a number of county operations, including animal control, HAZMAT, false alarm reduction, emergency medical services, and 9-1-1 operations. In addition, the Charles County Government operates an emergency operations center during severe emergencies activation at this facility. The authorized full time employee strength is one-hundred eighty-five. Most of those one-hundred eighty-five are assigned to staff ambulances or work in the 9-1-1 Center and they work a rotation shift. At any given time of day, sixty-five salaried employees would likely be on duty. These include volunteers and those salaried individuals performing their emergency response duties remotely through virtual connectivity. The critical 9-1-1 Center at this facility is in operation 24/7, and has immediate one-touch connectivity with all other 9-1-1 networks "All Call" with neighboring states during an emergency.

Tony amplifies this point. "Our 9-1-1 Center does have improved access to neighboring jurisdictions using dedicated communications circuits and public safety radio channels. 'All-Call' is a function within Charles County that we use to alert DES and volunteer Fire/EMS personnel. 'All Call' was created as a direct result of our response to the tornado."

This view inside the 9-1-1 Center was taken from the *Charles County Government Emergency Preparedness Guide* and not by the author himself.

10-7: *The 9-1-1 Center.*

The 9-1-1 Center is fully equipped with state-of-the- art communications and GIS technological capabilities and assets in order to insure optimum connectivity with the public and other 9-1-1 centers in its day-to-day activities, as well as during a severe emergency. The 9-1-1 Center transitioned to Next Generation 9-1-1 on October 21, 2021, which further enhances its wireless communication capabilities. The facility operates a mobile command center vehicle during an emergency in order to coordinate DES response activities with other mobile command entities, such as the Charles County Sheriff's Department. Tony adds this point. "This vehicle contains the technology that provides the opportunity for us to be interoperable with public safety response partners (9-1-1, fire, medical, law enforcement, incident management, public utilities, etc.) both in and out of Charles County."

Finally, the facility maintains twelve fully equipped emergency vehicles for their entire command staff, each tailor designed to meet the duty requirements of each senior staff member. That is, animal control, HAZMAT, 9-1-1, and so forth.

This Google map shows the location of the Charles County Government's Department of Emergency Services (DES), not far from Downtown La Plata.

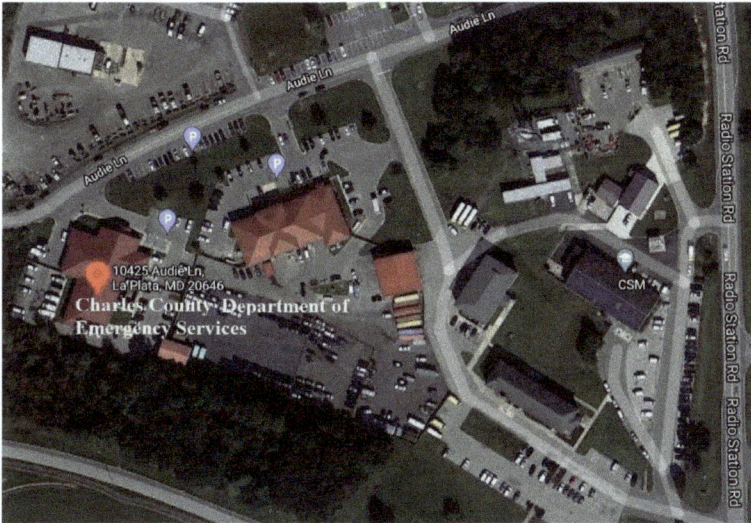

10-8: *The Location of the DES.*

The author took his photograph of the DES on the day of his visit to the facility.

10-9: *The Charles County Emergency Services Building.*

One of the loudest complaints heard during the entire cleanup process was that no alarm system had signaled the impending danger. **It is worth noting, once again, that the National Weather Service issued a tornado warning for Charles County only after it was already in La Plata, so an alarm system wouldn't have helped much.** Consequentially, on the night of the tornado, most residents just went inside their homes and into their basements because of the ominous clouds and the sights and sounds of wind increasing in velocity.

Immediately after the tornado went through, one of the companies that specialized in warning devices installed a siren in the center of Town as a demonstration project. The initial siren, a Whelen WPS-2805, was installed near the La Plata Court House, as seen in this Google Maps street panorama of Charles Street.

10-10: *Location of initial warning siren.*

A close-up of the Whelen siren is seen next.

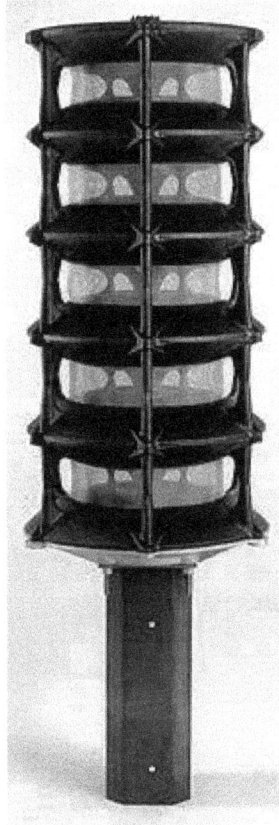

10-11: *The Whalen siren.*

The operation and testing of these warning sirens for the Town of La Plata is a collaboration between the Town of La Plata and DES' 9-1-1 Center. These sirens not only have the capability of emitting a loud tonal sound, but can also communicate a verbal warning over a speaker system in order to provide detailed information on what type of danger is imminent, as well as any location and urgency messages. After a number of tests, the Town installed another five sirens to provide coverage throughout the Town. These sirens are all solar powered and will continue to operate even if the electric system is destroyed. In the future, developers will be required to add sirens as part of the infrastructure when new subdivisions are in the planning stages.

To hear what one of these sirens sounds like during a test, go to:https://www.youtube.com/watch?v=ehy1ZznPQ44

The six sirens are installed at the following locations:

1) On Charles Street in front of the Charles County Courthouse.
2) On Curley Hall Road at the Town's Wastewater Treatment Plant (near Quailwood Subdivision).
3) In the Clarks Run subdivision.
4) In the King's Grant subdivision.
5) On Shining Willow Way next to the La Plata Volunteer Fire Department.
6) College of Southern Maryland.

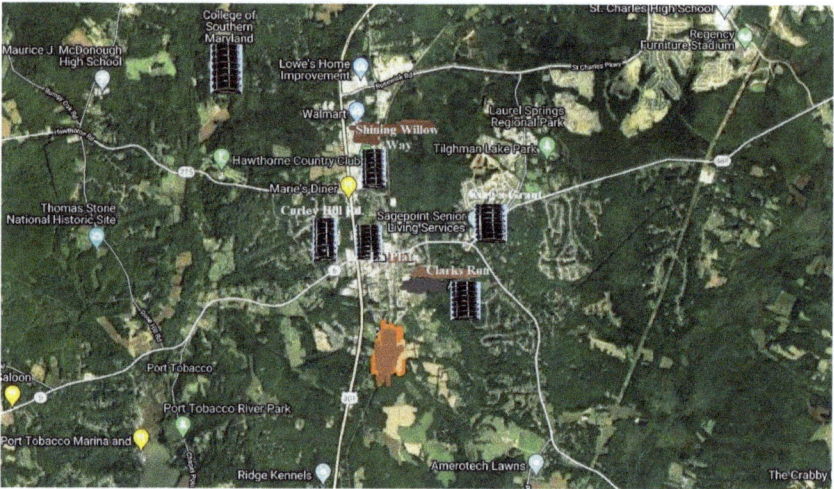

10-12: Location of warning sirens.

The testing of these sirens is done twice per year in early May and early December at 10:00 a.m. Public notification of these tests is made prior to the actual test, and testing lasts about a half hour. The following Tornado Warning Siren test notification sign is seen along eastbound Hawthorne Road (Maryland State Route 225) near La Plata, Maryland.

10-13: *Tornado Warning Siren Test Notification Sign.*

The tests consist of both siren alerts and audible notifications. One of the most dangerous places to be when a tornado strikes is in an automobile. The warning sirens will make motorists coming through La Plata aware of the danger, but there needs to be some place for them to take shelter.

A Federal Grant of $150,000 provided funds for a new police station, storm shelter, and Command Center for the Town of La Plata.

As part of the recovery from the 2002 tornado, the Town decided to convert the damaged Post Office building, located a few blocks from the new Town Hall, to the La Plata Police Department. A community meeting room was included in the police station and the decision was made to harden that portion of the building to withstand 170 mph winds and projectiles up to 110 mph. That room was also equipped as an Emergency Operations Center (EOC) that could be used by the Town to coordinate the efforts of the emergency services and the Town forces during major events. It can also serve as a backup to the Charles County EOC on Audie Lane after the immediate danger has passed.

10-14: **The La Plata Police Department.**

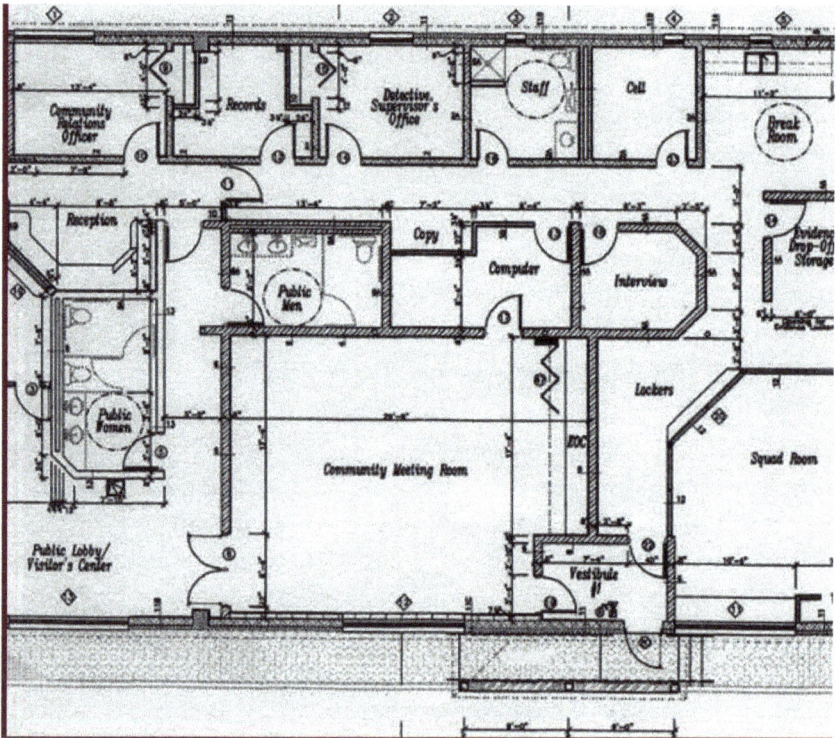

10-15: *Layout diagram of police station.*

10-16: *Storm shelter and EOC.*

10-17: *The community meeting room.*

The collapse of the old seventy-five thousand gallon water tank, leaving the Town without any water supply, was a horrible situation that needed to be corrected should another disaster like the one that happened in 2002, ever happen again. Thanks to $1 million grant from Congressman Hoyer's office, the seventy-five thousand gallon elevated water tank has been replaced with a seven-hundred fifty-thousand gallon ground level tank with booster pumps that maintain a good operating pressure throughout the Town.

10-18: *La Plata's 750,000 gallon water tank.*

In June 2017, the Charles County Government Department of Emergency Services published its **Emergency Preparedness Guide**, which provides valuable information dealing with planning for an emergency, the various weather hazards and other hazards, and emergency contact information.

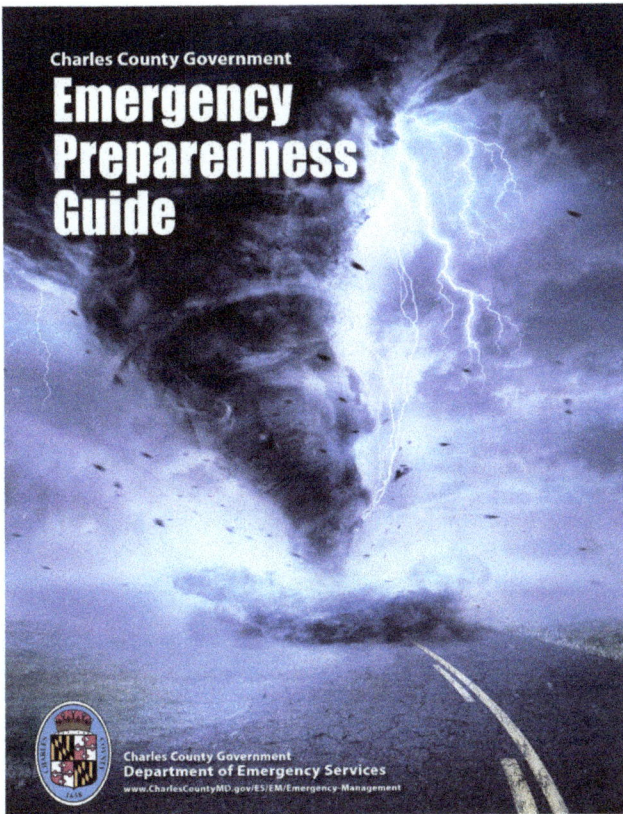

10-19: *The Charles County Government Emergency Preparedness Guide.*

CHAPTER 11
In Memorial

Lest We Forget
The Star Memorial Garden

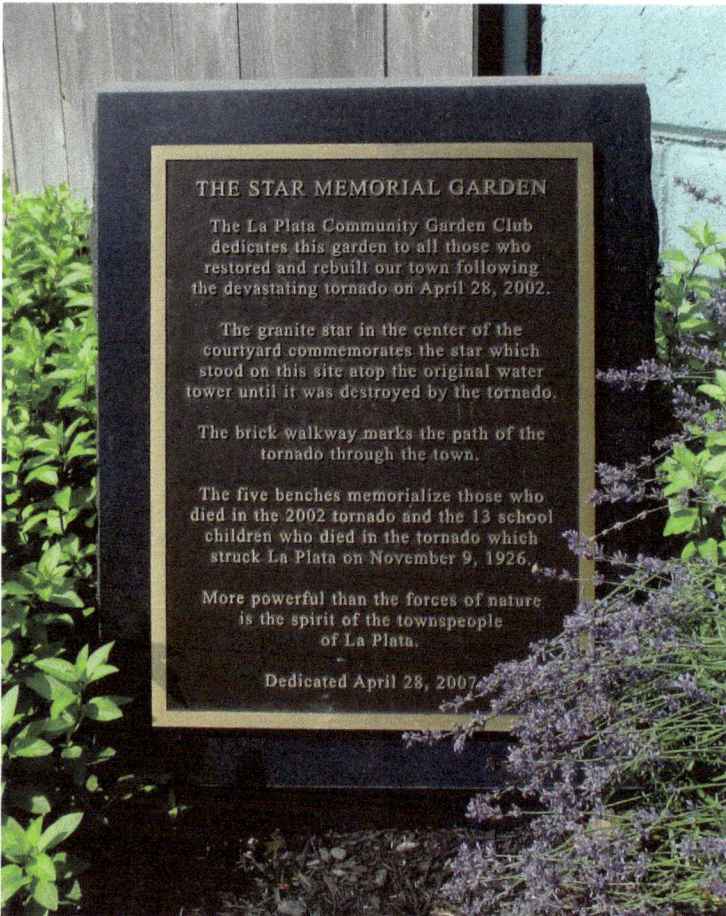

11-1: *Marker at the entrance to Star Memorial Garden.*

This marker is in La Plata, Maryland in Charles County. The marker is on Firehouse Alley 0.1 miles west of St. Mary's Avenue. The marker and the Star Memorial Garden are located behind the Charles County Board of Elections office at 201 Charles Street.

11-2: *Location of the La Plata Tornado Memorial Garden.*

On April 28, 2007, the La Plata Community Garden Club dedicated this garden to all those who restored and rebuilt the town following the devastating tornado on April 28, 2002. The granite star in the center of the courtyard commemorates the star which stood on this site atop the original water tower until it was destroyed by the tornado.

11-3: *Commemorative Star.*

The star mounted on a pole nearby is a symbol of perseverance rising above chaos and destruction.

11-4: *Symbolic star in the Memorial Garden.*

The brick walkway in the Memorial Garden traces the actual path of the tornado as it traveled through Downtown La Plata.

11-5: *The brick walkway in the garden.*

The original concept called for the placement of four benches at the Star Memorial Garden, which would memorialize the five people who died as a direct result of the 2002 tornado, as well as one bench to memorialize the thirteen children killed in the deadly February 9, 1926 La Plata tornado.

Two of the deaths on Sunday April 28, 2002, occurred in the La Plata area when the tornado touched down along Route 301 after shortly after 7 p.m.. William G. "Erik" Erickson Jr., 51, died when his unfinished house collapsed on him on Hawkins Gate Road.

11-6: Erickson bench.

A second man, Donald L. Hammonds Sr., 54, died of a stroke that he suffered while sitting in a car at the intersection of Routes 301 and 6.

11-7: Hammonds bench.

The final person to die in Charles County was Phyllis J. Taylor, 72, of Waldorf, who had a heart attack on Sunday, April 28, 2002, the day of the tornado.

11-8: *Taylor bench.*

In Calvert County, George Alvey, 68, and Margaret Alvey, 78, of Prince Frederick were killed when high winds picked up their small, unanchored farmhouse off its foundation and hurled it eighty-feet into a ravine off Route 231. Margaret died immediately in the home while her husband, George, was flown to Washington Hospital Center where he died the following Friday from his injuries.

FAMILY PHOTO

George Alvey, 68, died of his injuries yesterday. His wife, Margaret Alvey, 78, was killed in the storm Sunday.

11-9: Photograph of the Alveys.

Because the Alveys were originally from Calvert County, their bench was gifted to the Town of Prince Fredrick by the Town of La Plata. The Town of Frederick subsequently placed the bench at the King Memorial Park, located at 28 Duke Street in Prince Frederick, Maryland. As a point of interest, the Alveys are buried at the La Plata United Methodist Church Cemetery in Dentsville, Maryland, which is in Charles County.

11-10: *The Alvey's bench.*

One of these benches is dedicated to the thirteen school children who died in the tornado, which struck La Plata on November 9, 1926.

11-11: *The 1926 school children bench.*

The May 3, 2017 issue of the *Southern Maryland News* published an article written by Tiffany Watson entitled, "*Brand new sculpture in La Plata commemorates 2002 tornado.*"

On Saturday, April 29, 2017, at the Celebrate La Plata event, the town unveiled a fifteen foot sculpture created to commemorate the day the tornado stuck La Plata on April 28, 2002.

11-12: *The Star sculpture.*

"The Star sculpture stands as testament to the chaos that happened fifteen years ago. The star at the top highlights the rising of calm after the storm," said Judy Norris, chair of the Beautification Committee for the Town of La Plata.

The sculpture is located on Queen Anne Street in between the Sacred Heart Church on St. Mary's Avenue and the La Plata Town Hall and La Grange Avenue.Those who gaze at the sculpture will see black iron rods twisting upwards and finishing at the top where a silver star is the center of attention. The sculpture weighs two-thousand eight-hundred pounds and stands about fifteen feet high.

Norris said the sculpture had already been in the works since March 2016, with sculptor Lew Martin, owner of Indian Head Iron Works, and with guidance from the Beautification Committee. Martin, seen to the far left in the following photograph, was assisted in this project by Matt McCain, his apprentice welder at the Iron Works.

11-13: *The sculptor and his assistant.*

"The tornado means destruction — it's a destructive weather phenom," Martin said. "The star represents perseverance. It shows the strength and the will of the town, so I want everyone to concentrate on the star because we know we can defeat anything. The first tornado hit in 1926. The town came back and it happened again in 2002."

According to Martin, the entire sculpture is made of steel. The star on top is made of stainless steel with tubing around the star for added dimension. He said it took four attempts to get the sculpture right, but the effort was worth it because he loves the town.

"The sculpture represents for me and for others the twisted chaos the night that the tornado happened," said Councilman C. Keith Back. "I was Downtown walking the streets and there were places that I couldn't recognize — it was tough. The star represents the calm: the calm after the storm, the calm of the people that helped, the calm of all the citizens who joined in to make the town what it is today."

Councilman Joseph Norris said the star on the top of the sculpture reminds him of a similar one that used to be on the water tower before the tornado struck. "You could see the star on the water tower from a distance and know that you were getting close to home," Norris said.

Norris concluded, "The citizens of the town can marvel at the unique sculpture every time they walk by Town Hall."

11-14: *The sculpture and the Town Hall in the background.*

Once again, in the course of human endeavor, the sheer will of the human spirit prevails. As always, humanity in its bleakest hour will find solace in knowing that "Hope Triumphs over Chaos."

A child's bear is recovered in the debris of the tornado, reminding all of us that a cherished friend, once lost but now found, is a joy forever.

11-15: A reminder.

About the Author

Anthony (Tony) Puzzilla retired from the federal government in 2009 after forty-three years of distinguished service from 1966-2009. During his government years, the focus of his work was in the fields of disaster preparation, response, and recovery with the Departments of Energy and Homeland Security in affiliation with the Federal Emergency Management Agency.

He is now a full-time writer and lecturer. While employed at the Department of Energy, Tony became the Emergency Support Function (ESF) #12 - Energy chair at the Federal Emergency Management Agency (FEMA), beginning in early 1980, shortly after the agency was created in 1979. In this position, Mr. Puzzilla coordinated the deployment of ESF#12 personnel and assets to the disaster area, and kept FEMA informed of the "on the ground" activities of personnel as they interacted with the Energy Sector (electric power, crude oil, refined petroleum products, and natural gas).

Prior to an actual FEMA activation, including of course during the hurricane season, which produces not only tropical storms and hurricanes, but tornadoes when these weather systems made landfall, Tony was involved in hurricane tracking and monitoring, as well as daily briefings to high level personnel at the Department of Energy. When Tony transitioned to the Department of Homeland Security after 9-11-2001, he carried along the regular duties he already had with FEMA. He was very active in this position until he retired from government service in 2009.

During his tenure in the government sector, Tony became a very active member of the National Hurricane Conference's (NHC) Utilities Topic Committee. Within a few years of outstanding service on this committee, he became the Committee Chairperson. Eventually, Tony would be appointed to the Planning Committee of the NHC, while maintaining the position of Co-Chair of the Utilities Topic Committee. On April 24, 2019, Tony was awarded the Distinguished Service Award at the 2019 National Hurricane Conference for his "dedicated and long service, from 1980-2009, in supporting the deployment of energy personnel and assets to Presidentially Declared disasters."

Tony has been a resident of La Plata, Maryland, for 43 years and is a member of the Historical Society of Charles County.

This photograph of the author holding a photograph from his book was taken by Michael Reid, Community Coordinator for the Southern Maryland News.